Bringing Home the Cows

Growing up on a wild Devon farm

Bill Symondson

BⓑB

Brambleby Books Ltd.

Bringing Home the Cows: Growing up on a wild Devon farm
Text © Bill Symondson, 2023

A CIP catalogue record for this book is available from the
British Library

ISBN 978 1 90824 1672
eISBN 978 1 90824 1689

Cover design Tanya Warren, Creatix
Front cover image by Chris Wormell
Book layout by S4Carisle

Published 2023 by Brambleby Books Ltd., UK
www.bramblebybooks.co.uk

Printed by Lightning Source

In memory of Lucy

Contents

Contents

Contents

Prologue

This is the 'story' of one boy's life growing up on a farm in the 1960s. At the age of nine Bill and his family moved from the suburbs of London to a dairy farm near Torrington in Devon. They had no farming background and therefore everything was new to them, from how to milk a cow to getting familiar with the beautiful Devonshire dialect. The story is written as a series of vignettes, approximating loosely to the passage of time and tracking the changing mental development and interests of the boy. Thus, the writing reflects the initial naivety and lack of sophistication of a nine-year-old, but in a positive way. We are used to reinterpreting what young children and teenagers think, but here I have tried to capture his own changing perspective as he grows up. As an example, when he was getting excited about moving to the farm, he hoped that there would be lots of sheep that his dog Lucy could chase. Not an idea that would be shared by older teenagers or adults! In later parts of the book his older self has to negotiate his way through the complexities of relationships with girls, both the pains and the pleasures.

The 1960s are portrayed through a number of themes: the physical infrastructure (machinery, buildings), main farming activities (harvest time, milking), the domestic animals (especially the cows, chickens and ducks), pets (Lucy, the cats, guinea pigs, donkey, cage birds and more). In addition, a major theme is his interest in the wild animals sharing the farm with us, especially insects and birds. This theme in many ways defines the boy's character and is interwoven with all his other interests that charted his way through the rest of his life.

1
Lucy

It was about 4.30 pm and I was making my way home from primary school. It was a new school to which I had no affinity, and I was glad to get out each afternoon and head for the beech woods. I always came prepared with small jars and tubes into which I could put anything interesting that I came upon under stones and logs, or in the curled leaves on the bushes. There were mostly beetles, earwigs and centipedes, with caterpillars on the leaves in all their glorious diversity, imitating everything from multi-coloured toothbrushes to bird droppings. I couldn't take larger entomological equipment with me, such as a butterfly net. It would have been found and probably destroyed during the day by my delightful fellow students. Nor could I have visited the Butterfly Field, a small clearing in the beech wood that was humming with life on a warm day, such as this was, for fear that I would abandon all constraints and get my school trousers covered in grass stains and my socks prickly and stiff with the Velcro-covered seeds of goose grass and burdock.

After many diversions I reached the path that ran along the bottom of the gardens of Clifton Road, Chesham Boyes, where we lived. It was a sultry day and the sun shone down on the neat stripy lawns. People were sitting outside or gardening after work; it was a familiar scene that I had experienced many times, there was no presentiment of anything unexpected. This was the habitat of semi-professionals who liked their gardens to reflect the same ordered appearance as the rest of their lives. As I climbed over our garden fence, I saw that my mother and brothers were sitting on the grass and appeared to be waiting for me. This was a little strange. I didn't take much notice however, as I was keen to get home as I was, as usual after school, famished.

Then it happened. Out of nowhere there bounced into view a real, live, energetic golden retriever puppy. Where had it come from? Had a neighbour brought it round? The family were smiling like a row of Cheshire cats. I couldn't believe it. This wasn't happening. Nobody had mentioned a puppy. How was this possible? My brain couldn't keep up. She was a ball of golden life surrounded by a shock wave of my own adrenalin. This was Lucy, my most important and loyal friend and companion for the next twelve years.

2
Plans are Made

There is a lot to say about Lucy, indeed I could write a whole book about her and maybe there are some people who would prefer that to the tale I am going to tell you. Don't worry, Lucy will keep returning, like the good retriever she was. Lucy, from my nine-year-old perspective, was the pebble that in my mind started an avalanche of life-changing events.

My father was getting increasingly grumpy. His health was not good, and he did not get on with his brother in the family firm. Driving to survey ancient buildings across the length and breadth of polluted London caused him stress and headaches. He was a building surveyor looking for a change. Maybe he looked down one day at the model farms I liked to create, with plastic cows, sheep and horses, all sparklingly clean, on vivid green pasture with white picket fences. Later, and rather incongruously, I added rail tracks and a small green electric steam engine that used to race around the farm at a ridiculous speed. The farm animals took not the slightest bit of notice. But perhaps Dad did.

The next thing I remember is being taken to a factory farm. Dad was now the manager of ten enormous buildings, long and low, each one containing thousands of young chickens. Some of the sheds contained slowly flowing carpets of bright-yellow chicks, cheeping softly to each other. On one occasion we spotted a duckling, equally yellow, in amongst the chicks. I don't know what happened to it. As you moved from house to house, the chickens became larger and much noisier and apparently more aggressive. Subordinate chickens had half their white feathers plucked out and were a bloody mess. Chickens have sharp beaks, like hawks. The final house was empty. Fortunately, I did not experience the 'catching days', when they were all rounded up and had their necks pulled. Afterwards the silence in these empty sheds spoke loudly. Dad was not in this job for long. He had fought in the war, as a pilot, and maybe he had had enough of death.

There was a period when Dad was away for several days at a time. He would come back with multi-coloured pieces of paper on which were listed buildings and their dimensions, plus in some cases maps. There were no pictures, and it took me awhile to realise what they were. He had been away in the West Country obtaining details of farms that were for sale in Devon and Cornwall, and visiting ones that looked promising. Had he read my mind? Was he planning to move us all to a real farm? I started to look more closely at the co-loured sheets. The maps were of fields and orchards, the buildings were barns and milking sheds. These farms were enormous, rolling acres of mainly pasture. Could you actually buy such places? Dad did not have a farming background and now only knew a bit about chickens. Was he planning to cover such a farm in chicken sheds? Fortunately not, it seems. I noticed he was reading books such as *Farming for Profits*, *Farm Machinery* and *The Modern Dairy Cow*. It was going to be a dairy farm!

My mind went into overdrive. Think of all the wonderful wild-life that could be found on a farm, the birds, butterflies and crea-tures I had only ever seen on Brook Bond tea cards. Think of how Lucy would love it, racing around the fields and chasing sheep. Would there be streams and woods too? Would I get to ride on a tractor? Would I learn to milk a cow? Would Tulip, our tabby cat, be able to catch rats and mice, even rabbits? Would I be allowed to keep my own animals?

3
The Move

Time passed and nothing seemed to be happening. Maybe Dad had given up the idea of a farm and was now looking for a nice comfortable office job. Then suddenly there seemed to be a lot of boxes around and the house was in chaos. It was prudent to just keep out of the way as tempers were frayed. It was springtime when, unexpectedly, an enormous removal lorry rolled into our drive. Julian (my older brother) was staying behind with friends (to do his 11-plus exams), but the rest of us were packed into the Hillman Hunter. This included Dad, Mum, myself, Justin (my younger brother), Lucy, Tulip and my orange and white Guinea pig. The last of these we had recently bought at the annual end-of-year auction of school pets. He came with the unprepossessing name of Booboo, but, although I was only just getting to know him, he was the first animal (apart from the odd slug or spider) I had ever had that was unequivocally my own. I made a fuss of him therefore, ensuring he had food and water for the journey and that Tulip did not get too close. Tulip was tied into a cat basket and given a sedative. Lucy was supposedly confined to the back of the estate car but managed to smuggle her way onto the back seat before we had even reached the end of Clifton Road. Also packed into the car were boxes of delicate items which could not be entrusted to the removal van. Thus, we were bursting at the seams with very little room to move. A variety of organic smells soon accumulated from the animals (and people), getting stronger the further we travelled.

Today a trip from Buckinghamshire to Devon would not be considered much of a journey, but in those days it most definitely was. We had to stop off several times to allow the car radiator to cool down otherwise steam burst out from under the bonnet or (more scarily) into the car through the dashboard. The people, and Lucy, had to relieve themselves. This was not an option for poor Tulip, the danger of him escaping was too great.

Luckily Mum had packed a basket full of food for the journey and we picnicked in the fields along the way. We would turn off the main highway and find a suitable spot for all our needs. One such place was next to a field with two enormous old horses who took a great interest in everything we did. I hoped we would have horses on our farm, if not immediately then in time when we had settled in, in a month or so.

As any nine-year-old will tell you, sitting still in the back of a car for many hours is pure torture. Any activity (playing with a toy, humming a tune) was considered to be distracting to the driver and was quickly quashed. Normally. But this was not a normal journey. We were on our way to our very own farm. This made me see the passing countryside in a very different light. Would our house be like that stone cottage with a sagging roof? Would we have fields covered in poppies like that one? What colour would our cows be? As we got further and further from the Home Counties, the landscape got wilder. In the latter part of the journey, we crossed parts of Exmoor. Here the grass was coarse but dotted with patches of flowers and bright green mires. The sheep were shaggy and losing their winter coats. The horses were completely different from the two old fellows we saw earlier, much shorter and stockier, wild looking with their brown coats and long, black mains and tails. Was this where we would stop at our new farm?

Soon we left the moors of North Devon and came into the 'Land of the Two Rivers', the Tor and the Torridge. It was a country with small fields, bushy hedgerows and enticing woods. There were few arable fields but instead sheltered meadows full of content-looking cattle. There were lots of birds around, and kamikaze rabbits and pheasants on the roads. Our windscreen became clogged with dead insects. Clearly this was a land rich in wildlife and therefore perfect from my perspective.

Evening was coming on fast as we followed the River Torridge inland from Bideford then drove wearily up the steep Castle Hill into Torrington: behind us, to the west, there was a glorious sunset in the vibrant colours of butterfly wings – reds, oranges, yellows and pale greeny-blues. Such sunsets are perfectly normal in that part of Devon, close to the coast, but this first one was special and welcoming.

We stopped outside the Black Horse hotel in the town square, where we stayed the night. All of us, that is, except Tulip. Cats are a bit smelly after being confined in a small basket for so long and the hotel was not happy. So Dad took him to the farm, which was apparently just a couple of miles out of town, and shut him in one of the bedrooms for the night. There was one note of sadness that must be mentioned, a fatality. Booboo did not make it. Some-time during the journey he had tried to escape by sticking his head through a gap at the base of his cage. The luggage then shifted as we drove along and he was squashed. This was upsetting, but after I had shed a few tears, Mum promised to get me another one. The tears stopped. Little did anyone know at that time how Guinea pigs were going to become important in my life. I thank Booboo for that.

The next day the furniture would arrive at the farm, including our beds. I cannot remember anything else about our short stay in the hotel, probably because I, like the rest of the family, slept like a log despite all the excitement of arriving.

4

Arrival at Blackaton Farm

None of us except Dad had seen Blackaton Farm as yet. The house (a long red-brick bungalow with a conservatory on one side) was situated on a low hill looking down to the town and over the gently undulating Devon hills all around. Although it was a bungalow, it had five bedrooms, so we boys each had a room of our own. This was fortunate for everyone else because I was to rapidly fill mine with animals, both alive and dead. My brothers did not share my love of everything that could fly and crawl. However, that first day I kept out of the way again as our possessions had to be unloaded from the van and distributed to the right rooms. This was a good excuse to explore the farmyard, and I was set free to do so.

The farmyard was a short distance away from the house and located mostly in an old overgrown quarry. There were some solid buildings (cowshed, dairy, grain store, hay barn/implements shed and a silage clamp) containing a range of paraphernalia that I could not at first understand. There was also a motley shanty town of much older, farmer-built outbuildings, constructed of woodworm-riddled timbers, corrugated iron and slabs of rusty metal covered in rivets, apparently recycled from parts of ships. These rough old buildings were the bits I liked the best. They were like the farm buildings you see in old Westerns, except shabbier. It took me months to find my way into all the 'rooms', often by squeezing through gaps, crawling beneath floorboards or entering from above. Mostly they provided loose boxes for calves and cows that needed to be isolated in order to give birth in peace. There was an older disused cowshed, seriously decayed; entropy had had its way and the stalls were broken down or crumbling, home to sparrow, spotted flycatcher and swallow nests rather than to cows. To me this was a new world to be explored and was all terribly exciting.

I have to mention the smells. To a boy from Clifton Road the power of these farm fragrances was staggering. There was the expected smell of fresh cow dung, deposited by the milking cows as they visited the cowshed twice a day. This changed a bit from day to day, depending upon what they had been eating (grass, hay, kale, etc.). There was also the smell of the concentrates fed to the cows, and in winter sugar beet pulp. The latter smelt so good I could not resist chewing bits of the coarse cubes (they were deliciously sweet). Even the buildings each had their own smell that changed with the weather. Hot sun on corrugated iron roofs smelt very different to cold wet roofs. The outbuildings were a museum of smells going back decades. You could release these scents by pulling down a piece of woodwormy partition or better still digging in the accumulated dung and straw of a loose box that had not been cleared for a decade or more. Now there is an art to clearing out a loose box, only known to the initiated. First you need a special dung fork, wider than a garden fork with longer thinner tines. You then stick it into the dung at a shallow angle, lifting off the top layer. Only then can you get at the next layer. As you go back in time, the layers become more and more tightly bonded horizontally, so you end up ripping free sheets of the material that is more like large pieces of floppy carpet. But the surprise is that as you progress to deeper layers the smells change, indeed they get more powerful, more sulphurous. Basically, the bacteria change and those that can survive with little or no oxygen begin to dominate. The bouquet of all these smells can be overwhelming.

5

The Cows

Before going back to our first day on the farm, and Dad's first experience of milking, you need to know about the cows. From the time we arrived at the farm I developed a lifelong love of cows and don't quite understand anyone who is indifferent to them. Go into any field of dairy cows and sit quietly in the sun. At first, they will eye you up as they rip away at the grass with their tongues. Then they will gradually edge nearer to you, still eating away as if completely unconcerned and have better things to think about (like grass). Eventually the boldest amongst them will not be able to put up with this pretence any longer and extend their wet leathery noses towards you. You are expected to reciprocate by reaching out with your hand. The cow will give a quick succession of sniffs as it delicately dabs its wet nose against your fingers, then quickly pull away, curiosity satisfied. Another cow will then move in and go through the same process. You will be left with no doubts about the curiosity of cows or that there is a lot more to them than meets the eye. BUT, please do not go through this process if you have a dog with you. Dogs make cows frisky, and you might get accidentally trampled. It is also best to avoid cows with calves at foot; their maternal instincts may get the better of them.

Blackaton Farm was bought by us along with the previous farmer's cows and machinery. This was fortunate because Dad knew nothing about cows or how to choose a good one. There were about twenty of them, plus some in calf and younger heifers. The latter were sold off immediately as Dad wished to establish a flying herd. This rather strange term did not refer to their mode of locomotion or even their athleticism but simply to the practice of buying in replacements, as needed, rather than rearing our own.

The milking cows were a heterogeneous bunch which pleased me immensely. I had wondered before we moved what colour our

cows would be, but in practice our motley collection was every colour, shape, size and breed you could imagine. Many cows were
clearly crossbreeds and their ancestry was a matter of guesswork.
There were a few of the familiar black and white Friesians which
now dominate the industry, but they were not like the tall, rangy
Holstein-Friesian that you see today, rather these were dual-purpose
animals selected to be beefy as well as milky. There were also animals that looked a bit like Ayrshires, Guernseys and Devons. Now
Devons are not dairy animals but rather the local beef breed. They
are short-legged, fat, dark reddish-brown animals, which may have
been kept by the farmer before us as suckler cows. Dad didn't care
what breed an animal was a long as it gave milk. However, the 'Devons' were not what they seemed. One of these animals, called Titch,
was not giving much milk but, judging from her size, was eating a
lot of food. We decided to enter her for the annual show and sale
at Torrington cattle market. She won second prize in the Devon
section, but as there were only two entries to this competition, it
was not much of an achievement. We were also told that she was a
Redpoll, not a Devon. On top of that the cow went down with grass
staggers (a condition brought on by magnesium deficiency) during
the show, so we had to take her home again where she lived happily
on the farm for another year.

Of the remaining cows there was one group which was clearly
crossbred. In the post-war period dairy farmers were changing from
the traditional Dairy Shorthorns (brown, roan and white animals)
to the much higher-yielding Friesians. They did this through cross-
breeding, and the first crosses proved to be better milkers than either of the parent breeds. The offspring were easily recognisable
as they were usually blue and white. Three of these crosses (Ruth,
Bunny and Blackie) proved to be the best cows we ever had, thanks
to this hybrid vigour.

I should point out that we simply kept the names the cows were
given by the previous owner. The names (like Booboo) were not
particularly imaginative. When we bought in new cows, we were
able to come up with our own names. Once we bought a rather

ugly-looking, white cow (possibly an Ayrshire) that we called Puella. Strangely we discovered later that her previous owner called her Pugla, which actually suited her better.

We made the mix of cattle breeds on the farm even more complex through our choice of bulls. We did not keep one ourselves but rather used the AI (artificial insemination) centre which was just down the road. The obvious thing to do it seemed to me was to put a Guernsey bull to a Guernsey cow, an Ayrshire bull to an Ayrshire cow and so on. But as we didn't rear the calves, the only criterion that Dad considered to be important was the price we would get for the two-week-old calves at the market. At first, we therefore used the local Devon breed as the sire. If a Devon is crossed with a Friesian cow, the calf was almost always totally black. Black calves were popular with the buyers, and we got the best price from the farmers who wanted to rear beef animals. The problem was that many of our cows were brown and white, and this made the buyers suspicious. The calves from this cross were brown and an Ayrshire cross was less likely to grow up beefy. So, to outwit the buyers, we used Devons on the Friesians and Friesians on the Ayrshires, the latter producing black and white calves. This worked pretty well for a while until the buyers caught up with what we were doing. So we changed to using the Charolais breed, recently introduced from continental Europe. Charolais are massively muscular animals and produced beefy calves on any of the dairy breeds. They were also easy for the buyers to identify as they were white or cream. The beef-rearing farmers paid top prices for these calves. Unfortunately, the calves turned out to be too big. Our poor cows, especially the smaller breeds like the Ayrshires, had terrible problems giving birth, so we ended up using Hereford bulls on everything. Herefords are beefy animals and their signature white heads meant that the buyers knew what they were getting, whether the cow was mostly black or mostly brown.

Of course, cows that we bought in and which were already in calf produced offspring that were sometimes a complete mystery to us. One of the Guernseys we bought with the farm had a calf that was clearly the result of using a Jersey bull. It was the most beautiful animal I had ever seen, very small and doe-eyed, more like a deer fawn than a calf. Unfortunately, it was a bull calf and sold in the market for shillings rather than pounds. It is impossible to fatten one of these Channel Island breeds for beef.

6

Bringing Home the Cows

Very soon after arriving on the farm it became clear that there was one job at which I could excel. The cows had to be brought in for milking at about 5am and 4pm. I was excused the morning roundup, or rather I excused myself. Such an uncivilised hour was necessary to ensure that the milk was ready in time for collection of the churns by the local dairy. More importantly I could not be relied upon to wake up in time and, less importantly, would end up yawning my way through school classes. However, getting the cows in during a sunny afternoon was a joy. Often the cows had started to come in by themselves, as keen as I usually was for my tea. For them it was the lure of 'cow cake', the concentrates used to boost yield. At other times, if they were in a particularly lush field of fresh grass, I would have to roust them out. This involved a bit more running around, reminding them with shrieks of 'come on!' in my shrill young voice that they had a job to do and that I wouldn't stand for any nonsense. First though I had to find them, which meant learning the names of the fields. If I was told they were in Upper Newpark or Higher Hodges, then I knew I had plenty of time as they were not far from the house. Alternatively, they might be in West Graddon or Old Clover on the far side of the farm and more time would need to be set aside to allow for this.

Cows look enormous to a nine-year-old boy, and yet they don't take advantage of their size. They could easily turn back and decide not to bother with the inconvenience of being milked and instead browse happily on the mass of tasty fresh leaves and flowers in the surrounding hedgerows. But they didn't. Usually they were co-operative. The route back to the farmyard was most often through the cider orchard, with its maze of tracks between the trees, or via

Smully Ham beside the stream, and this did cause some loitering. But soon they would remember that delicious food was nearby (which might be eaten by another cow if they didn't get a move on) and the uncomfortable pressure of milk in their swollen udders would soon be relieved.

Although I took the business of being a cowboy seriously, I also found time to look out for interesting wildlife. There were butterflies everywhere, especially along the hedgerows. There were bird nests to spot, including the ground nests of skylarks and wood larks. In the trees were the great balls of prickly twigs occupied by magpies or the more open nests of crows. If I saw a pair of yellow hammers spending time in a particular stretch of hedge, I could go back later in the day and find their nest. Rough areas of field sometimes contained families of grey partridge, with their precocious chicks running around like bumble bees with invisible legs. Less attractive were the horse flies that swarmed on the backs of the cows but took delight in varying their diet by biting me on my exposed arms and legs. Swatting them roused my predatory instincts, especially if I managed to get them before they got me. Overhead were buzzards with their mournful cries, sailing effortlessly through the sky as they recalled the ancient landscape below that had changed little over the centuries.

7

Milking

So, having read up about dairy cows, how did Dad who had never milked a cow in his life manage to milk twenty of them on the day of our arrival at the farm and then again at 5am in the morning? Cows can be less co-operative than you might think and could deliberately sabotage the effort of anyone who clearly did not know what he or she was doing. The cows were tied up by chains to partitions down each side of the cowshed. Each cow knows its place and woe betide any cow that tried to change places. Thus, the cows were in pairs, with a small gap between them through which the person doing the milking has to squeeze. However, to a less bright (or less alert) cow this feels like another cow trying to encroach on its personal space. Both cows will then swing into action and press their bums together, closing off this gap. A lot of shoving and pushing will eventually convince both cows that the human in the cow sandwich means them no harm and that it is milking time. An experienced farmer knows that some gentle warning in the form of a few pats and verbal commands will prevent these battles that can leave the inexperienced wrung out, bruised and exhausted by the end of milking time. Equally risky is connecting the milking machine to the teats. If the cow has not been warned in advanced and feels something touching her teats, she may lash out with her hoof, either sending the machine unit flying or connecting with the offending person's leg.

So, how did Dad avoid these and other pitfalls that are unlikely to be found in books? Well, he knew what he knew and what he didn't. When he was managing that chicken farm, he met Bill Bailey who had some dairy farm experience. They came to an agreement and Bill Bailey and his family moved down to Blackaton at the same time as we did, taking a cottage near-by. This worked well for a time, and Dad learnt the basics of cow milking from day one. Bill was a bit of an enigma. He lived with his wife and another woman, much younger, in the same cottage. How this worked out only they knew, but they seemed to live in this three-way partnership quite amicably.

One day I was walking up to the farmyard with more exploration of the outbuildings in mind when my father came storming towards me with a face white with anger. Apparently, Bill was late with the evening milking and had blamed me for distracting him with my chatter. As I had not spoken to Bill all day, this surprised me. Dad took a swipe at me, but I ducked, and he missed. He then took another swipe and I realised that he would not be too happy if he missed again, so I let him hit me. It was a glancing blow that didn't hurt at all. That was the first and only time that my father had tried to hit me. I think it shocked him more than it hurt me. My opinion of Bill Bailey went down considerably.

8

The Reservoir

My most exciting discovery in those first few days on the farm was the Reservoir. To get there you had to follow the stream from the farmyard, up through Smully Ham, then over Town Meadow and Furze Hill. All three of these fields were popping with wildlife. What wildlife likes best is untidiness, and these meadows had been appropriately neglected for a very long time, with carpets of orchids in the spring, thistles much taller than me, ancient oak and ash trees along the hedgerows and a pair of barn owls keeping the voles in check. But the culmination of this pathway to paradise was the disused Reservoir itself. This was not strictly speaking part of our farm and had 'Private Property' notices to try to frighten me away, but I ignored these warnings for the next ten years and was never challenged.

It wasn't the lake itself that was the greatest attraction, although its five acres or so of sparkling water surrounded by water-loving plants were beautiful. And, although I was lucky enough to see a few ducks and grebes on the water over the years, it was too deep and hence cold to be appealing to much wildlife. The great attraction was the earth dam that retained the water, and the surrounding land. Neglect had been taken here to a higher level and the whole area was a riot of brambles, wild roses, stinging nettles, burdock, meadow sweet, fleabane and a hundred other species of plant, all buzzing, zinging and whining with insects, from gaudy butterflies to noon flies (big flies with orange wings).

Back in Buckinghamshire I had seen many of the commoner and ubiquitous species of butterfly, including meadow browns, ringlets, speckled woods, commas, red admirals, common blues, small coppers and peacocks. These (and their caterpillars when I could find them) were exquisite and totally wonderful, fostering an interest in butterflies that stretched back as far as I could remember. But even then, the excitement of seeing something new was intense. Two particular events stood out. The first was when I caught a white butterfly in spring with dappled greenish colouring on the underside of the hindwings. I feverishly looked through my butterfly books and for a few days was convinced that this was a Bath white, a very rare vagrant from continental Europe. Later I realised that it was simply a female orange tip, lacking the orange found on the male. I wasn't too disappointed. I had discovered for myself the interesting phenomenon of sexual dimorphism. My other rare sighting was of a white letter hairstreak sitting on a bramble leaf. There was no doubt about the identity of this one and the excitement was intense. I could think about nothing else for at least a month.

I discovered the Reservoir by chance, during my exploration of this massive piece of land that was our 82-acre farm. I could not quite believe that it was possible to actually own a large piece of the planet and everything on it. Did we own not just the grass fields but all the birds and insect too? Did the big trees belong to us? Or did they belong to no-one but just happened to live out their lives on our land? Did an owl or a butterfly flying across one of our fields belong to us in the same way as we owned Tulip and Lucy? Although I was only nine years old when I started to worry about this problem, I have never managed to get my mind around it. Perhaps there is a difference between owning something and having responsibility for it.

On the day I first discovered the Reservoir, I had my butterfly net with me, as usual, and Lucy, two essential elements to any expedition. Lucy was excellent at flushing insects out of the undergrowth. We pushed our way into the sea of prickly vegetation, and Lucy crashed through the nettles and brambles at top speed, hoping to find a rabbit. The air was filled with a swirling mass of bees, flies and butterflies and the heady scents of flowers plus the tangy smells of crushed vegetation. I was totally in my element. There was a primal quality to this place, and my brain responded to it in the same way that ancient hunter-gatherers must have done. In my case I was hunting butterflies rather than anything edible, but the excitement of the chase must have been very similar. Swinging a butterfly net over brambles was a delicate business as there was always the danger that it would get snagged on the prickles and possibly torn, which would be a disaster. I was able, more by luck than judgement, to successfully sweep up an orangey-brown butterfly that I thought must be a comma. With expertise acquired from much practice, I transferred it to one of my stocking-covered shoe boxes in order to get a good look at it. I was struck dumb with amazement. I had never seen a fritillary of any kind before, other than in books, but I knew immediately that that was what it was. This was intensely exciting. I had never in my most optimistic thoughts about our farm predicted that I would encounter such wonderful insects. I didn't know what species they were but could work that out if I took them home and looked them up. We stumbled on and it was clear that not only were there lots more fritillaries, but they were the most common butterflies on the site. After catching and releasing several more, I suddenly realised that the one I had just netted was different. Whereas the others were black and orange, in intricate patterns, with silvery patches on the underside, the new one was black, cream and orange. Into the shoe box it went. To have discovered one new species was extraordinary, to find two within a day was overwhelming. I rushed back home and pulled all my butterfly guides from the shelves. The commoner species I discovered (with some difficulty) were small pearl-bordered fritillaries, whereas the ones with cream cells were marsh fritillaries. But that was not the end of my list of discoveries. On subsequent visits to the Reservoir, I found brimstones, marbled whites, silver-washed fritillaries and walls, all new to me. Life at Blackaton was going to be exceptionally good.

9
Mum

While Dad was finding out how much work was involved with running a dairy farm and coming home filthy and bruised after every milking, Mum was finding that her rather romantic view of farming life was not quite what she had expected. There were three growing boys who managed to get all their clothes dirty within seconds. There were six meals to cook three times a day and all the washing-up to do by hand. There was a whole house to clean and an ancient coal-fired stove to keep fed. The latter had its name embossed on the front of the oven, the 'Ideal Cook 'n Heat'. It was not much good at doing either and gave so little heat that Tulip used to drape himself across the top and go to sleep. When he awoke, as the temperature crept up, one side of him would be ironed flat. Lucy and Tulip contributed generously to the mess. In Lucy's case that was in the form of large muddy footprints whenever she came in, especially after she had indulged in her regular relocation of her collection of bones, which she sometimes kept in the dung heap. She seemed to be more than a little paranoid about having her precious bones purloined by the farmyard cats. Tulip's contribution was more gruesome. He was very adept at catching young rabbits, always at night. He would bring them into the house and have great fun releasing them, thundering around the house re-capturing them and then torturing them, at which point they squealed like piglets. At 2am none of us was prepared to get up and deal with this, so we just had to bury our heads under our pillows and wait for him to finish them off. In the morning the whole house would be covered in fur and bits of rabbit guts.

Mum was also responsible for looking after the smaller farm animals. Beautiful white chickens (Light Sussex) were bought, with black feathering on their necks that lived free range in one of the orchards. They didn't realise that they should lay their eggs in the chicken hutch and instead made nests for themselves in the hedges. By the time we found them there would be a great heap of 20–30 eggs happily going bad. Gradually the hens disappeared as the fox got them. More chickens were bought, lovely gingery coloured birds (Rhode Island Reds x Light Sussex) and set free in the farm-yard. These birds sensibly roosted at night in one of the decrepit old buildings, where they spent the night too high in the rafters for the fox to bother them. These hens were just as capable of hiding their nests in the thousands of nooks and crannies available to them. When working at Bideford Zoo a few years later, I was given a pair of Red Jungle Fowl, wild ancestors of all domestic chickens. The cockerel had a piercingly loud crow; perhaps he used this to keep the domestic hens in order. As the summer progressed, the domestic hens hatched out dozens of chicks. Surprisingly, after only a week or so, these chicks developed feathers on their wings allowing them to fly after a fashion. Consequently, they got everywhere and just became a nuisance. The final straw was when they invaded the cow-shed during milking time, pinching the cows' food and spooking them. Dad decided they all had to go.

Mum bought some Khaki Campbell ducks too that comically rushed around, apparently on tiptoes. This upright stance is a result of their origins that included Indian runner ducks. They are noted for their amazing productivity, laying up to 300 eggs a year. We had a drake as well, but while the ducks incubated and hatched plenty of ducklings, the mothering instinct of the ducks was non-existent. They would take their newly hatched youngsters down to the stream and watch them floating away and out of sight around the bend. Far from being worried about this, the mother duck would completely forget about them. There was another farm about half a mile downstream, and the first time the farmer, Mr Hills, found one of these float-aways he brought it back to us in disgrace. The next day it disappeared again. We told the farmer he could keep any further duckling that might appear. The best thing about the ducks was their eggs, which, when fresh, were unbelievably delicious.

Mum was also responsible for feeding the calves twice a day. I don't think she enjoyed this very much. The cows had their calves at random at any time of the year, so that at any point in time there may have been none or three or four. The calves stayed with their mothers for their first day of life but then were taken away and bucket-fed. We kept them for a couple of weeks to toughen them up before exposing them to the rigours of one of the local markets. Calves are not stupid but give the appearance of being so. Instinctively they look upwards to try to find their mother's udder, and Mum had to persuade them to look down into a bucket of milk. The trick was to get them sucking your fingers vigorously, then push their heads down into the milk, gradually withdrawing your fingers. Most of them got the idea after a few days. The problem was that the calves got frustrated if the flow of milk into their throats was too slow. They would suddenly, without warning, buck their heads up, tossing the bucket and milk into the air. If Mum's fingers were in the calf's mouth at the time, this could be a painful as well as a messy business, especially when the calf had well-developed teeth, as many did. I used to help Mum with feeding the calves and rather enjoyed the battle of wills.

Mum was a marvellously artistic person who had been to art college, but she wasn't always entirely practical. On one occasion, soon after we had arrived in Devon, she got a large biscuit tin and packed it with moss. Into the moss she pushed some duck eggs, surrounding each egg with primroses, then parcelled it up and bravely took it all the way to her mother in Ruislip, Middlesex, on the back of her moped. What arrived was a raw and sticky version of scrambled eggs.

Although Mum had little time for anything other than house and farm work, she did try to find opportunities for us be creative and to learn how to follow more artistic pursuits. My favourite was papier-mâché. We could tear up newspaper, mix it with wallpaper paste, churn it into a grey mush and then mould it into whatever we liked. In my case I mainly made models of farm animals. The Ideal Cook 'n Heat came in useful to dry out our objects, after which we could paint them. We also learnt how to knit scarves, use a Knitting Nancy to create endless dressing gown cords, make rugs by hooking wool through canvass, mould objects out of clay, draw and paint. We would make delicate lampshades by blowing up a balloon, covering it lightly with oil, then sticking overlapping layers of coloured tissue paper onto it, again using wallpaper paste. When the glue dried the balloon was deflated and removed. When hung up with a light bulb inside, the effect was magical. I loved it all. A good proportion of our Christmas decorations each year were handmade.

10

Julian and Justin

There was surprisingly little overlap between myself and my two brothers in terms of our interests. Neither Julian nor Justin had the slightest interest in wildlife or farm animals. Julian liked mechanical things, such as building battleships out of kits or making constructions out of Meccano. He had a model steam engine powered by methylated spirits. He liked to use Dad's old enlarger to process black and white photographs. It was the process that interested him, not photography itself. He also had a telescope, but again it was the equipment itself that he liked. We did one day go to Tamar Lake and looked for water birds, such as shoveler ducks, something we both enjoyed but for completely different reasons. Justin was interested in meteorology and liked to record maximum and minimum temperatures. We all liked building bonfires, especially on Guy Fawkes night. We all also enjoyed tennis. There was an old court on the farm, covered in weeds and with broken-down fences. Dad had this professionally renovated as a proper hard court and we used to invite friends from school around to play on it. This was an unexpected luxury on a small farm. Julian was two years older than me and used to thrash me with his faster serves. Justin being three years younger than me, I was able to do the same to him. We soon learnt to play with friends rather than each other.

11

Old Farm Machinery

The long history of Blackaton Farm was recorded in several ways, but principally by the rusty, old implements, gradually turning to dust in the surrounding undergrowth. In the quarry itself, under a mound of brambles, were the remains of an apple press that must have been used at one time to make cider. It was probably driven by a horse, but the timbers from which it was mostly built were so decayed that it was difficult to tell. I liked the fact that, although the press had gone, the cider apple trees that supplied the fruit lived on in the adjoining orchard.

There was also a combined reaper/binder in Smully Ham, a very primitive forerunner of the combine harvester. Although it was a collapsed mess, you could still see the shape of it, even the iron seat where the operator sat. It was great fun to use the binder as a climbing frame, but bits were liable to break off it unless you were very careful. I particularly liked to sit quietly on the seat and absorb the atmosphere. The machine must have experienced hard times while the farmer worried about breakages, whether it might rain, how much cutting should be done leaving time for the sheaves to be set up into stooks before it got dark, hoping his wife would bring him something to eat and drink so that he could keep going (maybe fuelled by their own cider). These thoughts merged with an appreciation of what remained. The bits of wood and iron were laced together by brambles, thistles and tall grasses, which were in turn spun further into a mass of life by spider webs. I love the way nature can take back the crumbling works of men and women and make something beautiful out of the mix. I would listen to the ticking of the binder as it responded to my weight, which then combined with the buzzing of bees and grasshoppers and the whining of hoverflies. If I kept very still, I would often be joined by a wren, hopping through the mat of spars and weeds to find insects, some-times breaking into disproportionately loud and belligerent song. This was his territory, not mine, and he was going to make sure I knew it.

The real workhorse on the farm, and the only tractor we ever had, was an elderly Fordson Major. It had to do everything: plough-ing, rolling, harrowing, carting hay, muck spreading and much more. Dad spent a lot of time keeping it in good working condition. Unfortunately, he never let me drive it. When I was a bit older, he let me drive our Land Rover occasionally, years before I took my driving test, which was great fun. I did not find rolling a field after cultivation the least bit boring.

12

Old Blackaton

Old Blackaton was, after the Reservoir, one of my best discoveries in those first few days. Before our house was built this was the farmhouse, now long abandoned. To reach it you needed to walk through either Smully Ham or the cider apple orchard and into Town Meadow. The latter is a strange name for there is only one house with some small, saggy outbuildings around a tiny farmyard. The house nestled in a dip in the field at a point where three fields met. The house was built of cob, a mix of clay soil, sand, gravel and straw. There are more cob houses in Devon than anywhere else in Britain. The walls were exceptionally thick and, in the past, must have provided good insulation. Old Blackaton had just two small rooms on the ground floor with no windows. The cows used these rooms as shelter, wandering in and out as they pleased. There were no stairs. To get to the upper floor, you had to climb through a hay rack. As I could not imagine Dad trying to do this, the upper floor became my territory where I could be assured privacy when needed. It was one big room, open to the roof (now corrugated iron but probably thatched at one time). It had a small fireplace, suggesting that the farmer's family used this level as their home, while the lower floor was for livestock. A large hole in the wall must have been created in more recent time allowing the upper floor to be used for storing hay bales. It was probably hundreds of years old.

On the day I first explored this building I climbed through the hay rack and peered into this living area. Sitting on a wooden beam was a pair of barn owls, the female darker cream than the pale male. We looked at each other with astonishment and, although I held my breath to keep as still as possible, they both took flight silently and swooped out through a hole at the apex of the roof. On subsequent visits I climbed up as quietly as possible and stuck my head up slowly. The owls soon got used to this and accepted my visits, if not with equanimity at least with tolerance. When facing away from me, they would turn their heads 180 degrees, in typical owl fashion, to stare down at me with their enormous dark eyes. This was extremely exciting as I had never seen an owl of any sort before, although later I sometimes watched them gliding along the hedgerows hunting for voles. They nested in the chimney of the fireplace, which was blocked up with rubble. How they managed to get up and down the inside of the chimney to nest on the rubble I have no idea, but as they couldn't fly in such a confined space, I assume they used their beak and claws. Whenever I saw them, their feathers looked immaculate.

After we had been on the farm a couple of years a very different pair of birds moved into Old Blackaton, sharing the space with the owls. This was a pair of kestrels that nested on top of one of the walls. It was satisfying to see two predatory species living in apparent harmony. When the kestrel chicks were half grown, I started to handle them. They didn't appear to mind. I would put them on my arms or shoulders; they simply stayed put, not trying to escape. They had piercing eyes, hooked beaks and bright-yellow legs with dark and vicious-looking claws. They never attacked me in any way, and their claws were useful for holding on to my clothing. They only nested there for one year, but it was a memorable experience. I did a painting of them at school.

Old Blackaton was not a conventionally pretty place, with its stained walls, half smothered in ivy, and lack of windows. Nobody would consider renovating and living in it. The families of farmers who had spent their whole lives there were probably large, as was the norm, but there was very limited space in which to reside. But like the old machinery, Old Blackaton had in its latter years given in to the processes of decay, making a pact with nature to create a more restful environment. It would leave behind the ghosts of the people who had had such a hard life working the fields and raising sheep, cattle, horses and children.

13
Blackleg

Blackleg was one of the younger cows that we bought with the farm from the previous owners, the Parnells. She was a feisty animal with wickedly curved horns that she was not afraid to use when annoyed. She was almost entirely black and difficult to spot at night, not a good combination. One stormy and freezing cold night in the middle of winter she managed to break out of the farmyard.

There was snow on the ground, but the wind was blowing strongly, with heavy showers of freezing sleet. She was also heavily pregnant, so we couldn't just leave her out in the fields, not only for the sake of the cow but also in case there was a calf. So Dad decided, even on this pitch-black night, that we had to go out and look for her. With the help of just one dim torch between us we were able to pick up her trail in the snow. Cows have a map of their farm in their heads and will often seek a particular place where they wish to give birth. Such places can just be a corner of a field where there is shelter from the wind or within a small copse. We followed her trail across Hodges Down and on into High Hodges. Unfortunately, as these two fields did not have an open gate between them, she decided to jump over a strand of barbed wire that ran along one side of the hedge. She had clearly injured herself in the process for there was now a trail of blood as well as hoof prints to follow. After Higher Hodges she crossed the boundaries to Little Down, Well Moor and finally Higher Long Field.

It became clear that, rather indirectly, she was heading for Old Blackaton. The ground there was all churned up and it was impossible to distinguish her trail. By now we were all drenched by the sleet and tired from the yomp across the farm, not to mention scratched and battered as we tried to follow her through several hedgerows. As soon as we stopped, the cold wind ensured that the damp from the sleet and our own sweat made us feel colder still. Blackleg was particularly aggressive when she had a calf to protect, and we knew that she may have given birth. Somehow, blundering around in the pitch-black night, we had to look for her in the old farmhouse and the decrepit outbuildings at the back. Susan, who was employed to do the milking at that time, decided to try the old farmhouse. Almost as soon as she stepped in the front doorway she was suddenly bowled aside as Blackleg charged past her at high speed. Unfortunately, outside the front of the building was an old well, not very deep but deep enough to ensure that the icy waters poured into her wellies when she fell in. Fortunately, she wasn't injured. Blackleg meanwhile disappeared into the blackness. We crept around the buildings, terrified that one particular blob of darkness could at any moment resolve itself into a charging black cow. After several further mostly mock charges (she was a little deterred by our shouts and screams) we found out why she was being so aggressive. In one of the lean-to buildings (little more than one wall and a sagging roof) we found that she had given birth to twins, which were unfortunately both still born. After some consultation we decided that it was much too dangerous to continue, and that we had no chance at all of getting her to leave her calves without one or more of us being seriously injured. As there was no need to worry about a live calf, and we were all already suffering from hypothermia, we limped home.

The next day Blackleg was brought back to the farmyard. She still made life difficult by trying to double back and return to Old Blackaton, but her heart wasn't really in it. Perhaps she had come to accept that her calves were dead. In the end the dead calves were put into the back of the Land Rover with the back door open, and once she had had a good sniff at them, she followed us back to the farmyard like a lamb.

Meanwhile I went down with pneumonia. This was a bit scary, because at times I could hardly breathe, and the doctor was called. However, I was still enormously excited by the night-time adventure and this (plus glasses of blackcurrant Ribena, which we were only given when we were ill) got me through.

Shortly after this episode Dad got the vet in to remove the horns from all the cows that had them. It is rare for a cow to try to get you with the points of its horns, rather they were likely to hit you accidentally with the sides of their heads when you had to work at close quarters. They had no compunction, however, about butting other cows, for example when a cow didn't quite know its place in the pecking order or tried to squeeze into the wrong stall in the cowshed. This could cause injuries, often to new cows that had just been brought into the herd. The horns were removed with a cheese wire, a process that they did not enjoy. I was happy to take possession of the horns. My aim was to make some old-fashioned drinking horns, but I never found out how you remove the inner core of bone. Cows definitely look better with horns on, but I accepted that they had to be removed. Cows like Blackleg look rather forlorn without their head decorations, they lost their dignity and grandeur. For several days after horn removal the cut end leaked a greenish fluid plus some blood, which ran down their faces. These days the horn buds are usually removed from calves using a quarterising tool or acidic disbudding paste, a much less traumatic process.

14

Susie-two

When you are running a flying herd, it is important to keep up the productivity of the cows by both buying in high-quality animals and selling those that were not giving sufficient milk. One autumn it was decided that two animals, a Friesian (Susie) and a Redpoll (Tina), were not pulling their weight, both giving less milk than expected at that stage in their lactations. As they were in calf, it was decided to keep them until they gave birth and then sell them as dairy animals at Torrington cattle market. So instead of allowing them to munch their way through lots of hay in a nice warm barn with the rest of the cows but giving us nothing in return, they were turned out into the fields for the winter. All the gates across the farm were left open so that they could wander wherever they wished, grazing whatever they could find in the fields and hedgerows. In very harsh weather they came back of their own accord to the farmyard and were given a little hay. It was an experiment that had several interesting consequences.

First their appearance changed remarkably. They grew long, thick fur coats in response to the cold, rain and snow. They were almost unrecognisable. Secondly, despite the poor diet, they grew, if not fat, into animals clearly in very good condition. But the thing that pleased me the most was that they calved with no difficulty. One of those calves we named Susie-two (spoken as one word). This was the smallest calf I have ever seen. As the farmers say of such animals 'you could carry it in a bucket'. I pleaded with Dad to let me keep her and surprisingly, after some thought, he said yes. Although the calf was perfectly healthy, it was so small that nobody would buy it at the market.

The deal was that I should feed this calf and look after it in every way. Three other heifer calves were born at about the same time as

Susie-two, and it was decided that all four should be reared as herd replacements. This does not conform to flying herd principles, but again Dad was experimenting. So, there were three Friesians (Susie-two, Lorna and Pandora) and one pure Ayrshire (Poppy). Cunningly, Dad insisted that, as I was rearing Susie-two anyway, I could look after the other three as well.

Given a free hand, the first thing I did was teach Susie-two to walk on a halter. She resisted at first, but I gave her no choice; it helped to have an animal so small that resistance was useless. We used to go everywhere together, including up to the Reservoir where I could tie her to a tree while I scouted for butterflies. She clearly liked these walks and would get skittish, like a dog, when she saw me coming to get her with the halter. She grew rapidly until she reached a size when skittishness involved pushing me around. One day this became too much, and our walks had to come to an end. She grew into a large cow and at around two years old gave birth to an Aberdeen Angus cross calf and joined the milking herd. It is interesting that such a tiny calf should grow to normal size, probably because she was initially affected by the harsh life that her mother experienced out in those cold winter fields. It was a case of nature (her genetics) winning over nurture (a tough early life).

15

Primary School

I don't want to say too much about school, but the first one wasn't too bad, the second was awful and the third was the best. The first was a primary school in Torrington. Mum chose it because the headmaster said he was interested in butterflies, although there was not much evidence for this. He did introduce me to an old man who had cases of tropical butterflies and, although I liked them, I only visited him once. Far better was the fact that we older boys and girls were allowed out onto Castle Hill at lunch time. This was a precipitous slope running down from the back of the school to the River Torridge. It was covered in bracken, gorse, brambles and thorn bushes and was a great place for small pearl-bordered fritillaries. There were piles of grass clippings dumped over the castle wall from the bowling green. This grass heated up like a compost heap and every summer young grass snakes hatched out from this perfect incubator. The white band around the necks of these lovely snakes convinced the other pupils that they were adders, so they were killed on sight. I tried to persuade them that this was not the case, that they were perfectly safe and could be handled gently, but to no avail.

In class, I was mostly left alone by the teachers, even though they must have seen that I took little part in the tasks set for us. I was teased a bit for my home counties accent. At the beginning I found it hard to understand what the other students were saying in their rich Devonshire drawl, but in time I managed to emulate it.

One thing I was asked to do, and greatly enjoyed, was to paint directly on the classroom wall, a larger than life mural of the Pied Piper of Hamlin surrounded by rats. I really went to town on the rats, painting black rats and brown rats (because I knew there were two species), and rats of all sizes. I am still pretty good at painting rats, perhaps because I encountered them frequently on the farm, even in my bedroom. The rats never came up onto my bed fortunately, at least not while I was in it, but they did keep me awake trotting around my room in the middle of the night. I found some rusty old gin traps hanging on the wall in Old Blackaton. One night I set a couple with cheese as bait and went to sleep. At about 2am there was a heart-stopping crash as one of the traps was sprung, followed by a loud squeal. The trap had not caught a rat but did take a pinch of fur. The rats learnt their lesson from this experience and never returned.

There was a girl, Shelagh, from a large Indian or Pakistani family, who tried to be friendly with me. I had no experience with girls and so tried to discourage her. She was persistent, however, even offering me some of her food at break times. I think in retrospect that she too felt like the odd one out (there were no other families of South Asian origins in the town) and she recognised myself as another misfit (with my strange accent). I threatened to bring some scissors to school and cut off the plat down her back binding together her long hair, but she didn't take this threat seriously.

Once a year the town went a bit mad and held Mayfair celebrations and a carnival. The whole thing was delightfully pagan and involved the crowning of a May queen. The primary schools played a major role in all this. We learnt to dance around maypoles in the town square, holding coloured ribbons that formed different patterns on the poles, depending upon how we danced and wove between each other to music provided by the brass band. The worst bit was when we were paired up in a long line, boy partnered with girl, with our arms around each other, then danced around the town square in a long snake. The year I did it I was partnered with Shelagh (of course) and we led the procession. I had very mixed feelings about this, which I didn't understand. On the one hand I had my arm around a girl (gross!), while on the other hand I sort of enjoyed it and was feeling proud. She frequently looked up at me, smiling, and I found that I liked to smile back at her.

There was always a funfair to accompany the Mayfair celebrations, and this I did enjoy. There were dodgem cars, roundabouts and all the usual things. In one game you had to throw ping-pong balls and try to get them to fall into glass jars. The prize was a goldfish, and I invariably spent more money on this than it would have cost me to buy a goldfish in a shop. I kept one such goldfish in the well at Old Blackaton and it grew so fat that it ended up the size and shape of a large orange. I assume it lived on water fleas and mosquito larvae, plus the bits that got washed off the noses of the cows.

My main problem was the bus that took the kids who lived on outlying farms to and from school. The same bus transported the much bigger teenagers from the town's Secondary Modern School too. There was one boy who liked to push his hand up my shorts and grab my private parts. Once he had me in his grip, I couldn't pull away for fear of hurting myself. Today that would be classified as sexual assault. I couldn't tell my parents about this; it was too embarrassing and might lead to further unpleasantries. I decided instead to walk the two miles to and from home, whatever the weather, and avoided the bus completely.

This walk was no problem at all for a budding entomologist. I would look out for the folded leaves created by the larvae of micro-lepidoptera. Sometimes I found tortoiseshell and red admiral larvae on stinging nettles, which I took home and fed until they pupated. Watching those colourful butterflies hatching from the chrysalises was to experience one of the great mysteries of the natural world.

On one occasion at this school I did manage, inadvertently, to mortify my parents profoundly. The school had organised a day trip to Paignton Zoo in South Devon. My first thought was one of delight; I loved zoos, and this was a big one. My second thought was that, during these early days at the farm, we were very hard up and any income from the milk had to go towards building the farm into a successful concern. I therefore did not give my parents the letter from the school telling them about the trip and how much it would cost. I thought that if I gave them the letter, they would feel obliged to pay for the outing, even though they couldn't really afford it. So, I and two other boys didn't go on the trip. Instead, we three were asked to write a poem about anything we liked and mine was as follows:

Me, Alan and Jimmy
Must have looked very silly
Thinking of you
At Paignton Zoo
And not knowing what to do.

At break time
It was not in our line
To have no one to play with at all
So, as we were the tallest
We looked after the smallest
Until it was the end of our time.

Inevitably Mum and Dad discovered what I had done and found the whole thing very embarrassing. Surprisingly they were not as cross as I had expected, and a few weeks later took us all for a day out at Paignton Zoo.

Nevertheless, I did participate in another highly enjoyable school activity. This was a cycling trip led by the headmaster, staying overnight in youth hostels. I had never done any long cycle rides before, nor had the other children who participated, so we were advised in advance to do some practice rides of increasing length to build ourselves up for the expedition. I did a single practice run from the farm to Weare Giffard and back (maybe 15 miles), but no other preparation. As a result, I suffered for it, at least in the early stages. The first leg of the trip started with a 40 mile ride from the school down to Boscastle, then on successive days to Tintagel,

Launceston, Tavistock, Okehampton and then home. It was pretty tough going at first and we all got saddle sore. However, the landscapes that we went through, down the North Devon coast and then skirting the edges of Dartmoor, were wonderful. The best bit was Boscastle and Tintagel, which are close together and therefore gave us a rest after the long cycle ride the day before. We absorbed the local legends about King Arthur and did some exploring along the rocky beaches. There was lots of wildlife, from the whirling flocks of seabirds to the rock pools, with their multi-coloured anemones, crabs and blennies. Later we saw Dartmoor ponies and were accompanied by soaring buzzards with their evocative, but rather sad, cries. Needless to say, I was frequently diverted by the butterflies along the hedgerows and sunken lanes, including holly blues, which we didn't get on our farm.

The time came for me to do my 11-plus exams. As I was still only ten and had changed school three times in as many years, I probably hadn't learnt much. Anyway, the venue for doing the exam was the Secondary Modern School. While we were trying to concentrate on the exam questions a gang of large teenagers decided to bang on the windows and make faces at us. I was terrified that they would come in. Not surprisingly I failed.

16
The Buzzard

At the base of the Reservoir dam were two old concrete tanks sunken into the ground, probably containing in the past either some sort of filtration system or simply acting as holding tanks for water. By the time we were farming there, these structures were too decayed to have any useful function. With some difficulty (the walls were much taller than I was) I could get inside with the help of some drainpipes. The accumulated debris at the base fostered a whole community of flowering plants that were rather different to those on the dam, more delicate species that could thrive away from competition by brambles and choking grasses. These in turn were very attractive to butterflies and other insects and therefore a hot spot for my activities. Different species of butterflies dominated at different times of the year, so there were times when the majority were fritillaries (June) and other times when they were mainly marbled whites (July).

The tanks also operated as giant pitfall traps for anything that could not fly, such as hedgehogs and rabbits. I would rescue some of these if they allowed me to catch them. On one occasion I killed and took home a young rabbit that Mum skinned and cooked for our supper a couple of days later. As the soil in the tank was not very deep, these trapped animals could not escape nor avoid being spotted by predators, which probably took most of them.

One day I visited the area after a period of heavy rain. There was about a foot of water in the tanks which had probably drowned most of the small mammals. However, on this particular day something much larger was struggling in the water. It was a full-grown buzzard. It was completely saturated with water and had its wings spread out over the surface trying to keep afloat. When it saw me, it tried to escape, splashing around in an attempt to fly. It could not get out. Even if it had managed to get airborne, the walls were too close together for it to attain a flight trajectory that would allow it to escape, weighed down as it was with wet feathers. It was obvious that the more it struggled, the lower it floated in the water. Drastic action was needed in a hurry if it were to be saved.

I ran all the way home, dumped my usual insect collection kit and dug out instead a sturdily built shrimping net. I had to persuade Mum that this was an emergency that required her immediate help. She was not keen. I appealed to her good nature by telling her that she would be responsible if the buzzard drowned. She relented and we both rushed back. I climbed into the tank with the shrimping net and then paused. This was a magnificent and powerful predator which, if I was not careful, could easily lacerate me with its claws and beak. I managed to get the net under it and lift it clear of the water. It was surprisingly heavy, not helped by the weight of the water. It decided not to stay on the net but instead to walk up the pole towards my hands. I quickly lifted the now-vacated net end towards Mum who grabbed it, with a few anxious moans, allowing me time to climb out of the tank and come to her rescue. I lifted the end of the pole and carried it over my shoulder with the buzzard only a couple of feet from my ear. Fortunately it cooperated, and we were able to take it out into middle of Furze Hill and put it down on the grass.

I stayed with the buzzard for an hour or so. A lot of water dripped from its feathers, aided by its attempts to preen itself. It tried a short flight but soon crashed to the ground again. I decided to leave it to recover as it was clearly strong enough to survive. I felt extremely happy to have been able to rescue such a magnificent creature. Buzzards were quite rare at that time in Devon. They were sometimes seen eating dead lambs and accused (wrongly) of killing them and subsequently persecuted. They do, however, kill and eat young rabbits, which are pests of cereal crops, so should surely be conserved.

17
Guinea Pigs

Following her promise to me that she would replace Booboo, the Guinea pig that died on the journey down to Devon, Mum bought me (after a few reminders) a female brown Agouti, which I named Gangie (pronounced as in the River Ganges). This was the Eve of a dynasty, for all the Guinea pigs that I bred in subsequent years were descended from her. She was already pregnant when we brought her. She was very tame, and I fell in love with her at first sight. The Agouti colouring means that the hairs were bicoloured, giving them a ticked appearance. Agoutis are also a particularly large breed of Guinea pigs. She gave birth to two male offspring with the imaginative names of Blackie and Brownie, who grew to enormous sizes. Brownie was also an Agouti, looking very much the same as a wild Guinea pig. When the two males started to get aggressive with each other I left Blackie with his mother and moved Brownie to another cage. More babies were born to Gangie, mostly black. As these youngsters grew up, further incestuous offspring were born. There were no signs of loss of vigour, but I did eventually realise my mistake and bought in a couple of unrelated males, one solid gold in colour and the other black with long, rosetted fur. I became very interested in how crossing Guinea pigs of one colour or fur pattern with partners that were different would turn out. For example, most of the offspring of a cross between a brown Agouti and an all-black male resulted in black or brown offspring. However, completely unexpectedly, one beautiful baby was born blue Agouti, like a Shorthorn-Friesian cow, with patches of pure white. Probably all the inbreeding resulted in expression of recessive genes (I learnt about this at school).

My Guinea pig herd expanded rapidly, and I took over completely the shed that had been used as a store for garden tools.

I started to export youngsters to a pet shop in Bideford at five pence each. I fed them all on the concentrates that Dad mixed for the cows, supplemented mainly with grass. I don't remember ever having a health problem with any of my Guinea pigs other than needing to cut their claws from time to time.

Lucy and Tulip had an uneasy relationship with the Guinea pigs. Tulip liked to sit on top of runs that I constructed, which allowed the Guinea pigs to crop the grass directly. He couldn't get his paw through the netting. Lucy on the other hand seemed to think that it was her job to protect the Guinea pigs from Tulip, and so she lay down beside any run that Tulip was sitting on. No harm ever came of this interest.

To save time in the evenings, I used to collect bundles of grass from the hedgerows as I walked home from school. These I tied together with rush stems and hung them around my belt. The Guinea pigs were always very keen to welcome me home. As I got closer, I would call out to them, saying things like, "Are you hungry Guineas?" to which they would reply with a chorus of oinks. "Would you like some nice fresh grass?" "Oink, oink, oink." "Have you been good Guineas?" "Oink, oink, oink." "Should I sell you to the pet shop?" "Oink, oink, oink." It didn't matter what I said, they would reply enthusiastically. It gave me a really warm feeling to be welcomed home in this manner.

18

Harvest

Hay harvest was a time of great tension. We did grow crops occasionally, such as kale for winter grazing behind an electric fence and barley for rolling to form the basis for the concentrate mix given to the cows. The barley was harvested by contractors with a combine harvester. The grain went directly into sacks, which were horribly heavy. The whole family helped to load the barley onto a trailer and unload it again in the grain store. These sacks of barley were emptied during the winter into a mill driven by a belt from the Fordson Major. The straw was bailed by one of our neighbours (the Hills) and stored in a barn as winter bedding for the cows. We did have a purpose-built silage pit, and one year Dad had a go at making some. Unfortunately, we didn't get it right; the exclusion of air from the clamp was incomplete and the grass overheated, turning it all to ash. We didn't try again.

By far the biggest and most important harvest though was the hay. We invested in machinery to do this, including a tedder, to fluff up the cut grass and help it to dry, and a four wheel hay rake to scrape the finished hay up into windrows (a row of hay raked up to dry), prior to bailing. Dad would find the whole process so stressful that most years he developed a high fever and took to his bed. This was thought to be something to do with a tropical disease he may have contracted during his time as a pilot in Burma during the 2nd WW. We three boys were taken out of school (this was considered normal at harvest time and the schools did not object) and had to do most of the work, with help when possible from Mum and the current dairy man or woman. We loved the whole thing. Stacking the hay bales on the low-loader was the tricky bit. The bales were quite heavy and had to be passed up to the top layer in a series of steps; it took two people for each bale. In the early days the hay would fall off the trailer regularly on the way back to the farmyard. We soon learnt that tying everything down with ropes helped a lot, and Julian (with his usual interest in technical matters) learnt how to apply the special knots that allowed the ropes to be pulled tight and not come adrift. The fun bit was riding back on the top of the load, helping to hold in place any bales that were threatening to fall off. If the whole lot did roll off, despite our efforts, then we tumbled down with the bales. This too was great fun; no one was ever hurt. Re-stacking the trailer (often on a slope) was less fun. Storing the hay in the barn was very hard, sweaty work. In the early years we had to form a chain to pass the bales to the top of the heap, which was backbreaking. Eventually we bought an elevator which made it much easier.

The most stressful bit was getting the timing right. If rain threatened before the hay was cut, we could delay harvest for a few days. Once the hay was cut there was no going back. The hay, lying on the ground, needed a lot of tedding to get it dry again after a shower. Further rain might then be forecast, and it would be a race against time. If you baled the hay when it was too green it would go mouldy, the same for wet hay. The longer you had to work the hay to get it dry, the lower the quality of the hay. We lost completely a couple of fields of hay over the years, which was a big financial loss as we then had to buy in more to keep the cows going through winter.

Mum used to make elderflower champagne and home-made lemonade for the hay harvest period. Both smelt as delicious as they tasted and ensured we didn't become dehydrated, especially on hot days. The fresh hay smelt wonderful, too, the smell of summer. When we broke open the bales to feed the cows on cold dark winter evenings, hints of that summer smell would waft up and remind us of those sultry days.

Nobody had heard about sun cream at that time (at least we hadn't). As a result, we got badly burnt, with faces and arms becoming lobster red. This faded with time as the outer skin peeled off leaving a soft tan. Our palms also had to recover. Lifting heavy bales by their strings soon caused blisters if you didn't have leather gloves (which we didn't). I used to pull out handfuls of hay as padding for my fingers, which helped a bit.

Overall, hay harvest was for me the highlight of the farming year. Lucy had a good time too chasing any rabbits and partridges that were sheltering within the windrows. She also liked to follow the machinery in the field and then shepherd the trailers of hay down the road and back to the farmyard. I think she thought she was in charge of the whole operation.

19
Lucy (Farm, Coast and Woods)

Lucy took her responsibilities very seriously. If I happened to be in the house or doing something uninteresting (in Lucy's view) near to the house, she would lie Sphinx-like in her favourite spot on the top of the garden wall. This vantage point gave her a clear view of the back door (in case I came out) and down the drive (in case any strangers arrived). If the visitor was a man, she would start barking to give us advance warning. If it was a woman, she just wagged her tail and waited to welcome her in. I cannot remember her ever getting it wrong. Possibly she had been treated badly by a man when she was a pup, although that seemed unlikely. Who could possibly mistreat a seven-week-old golden retriever puppy?

Perhaps having spent her first year of life in a suburban garden she was not inclined to wander off on her own. However, it only took a slight wave of my hand for her to rush to my side and bounce around ecstatically. She would also jump up when our car was returning from somewhere, long before any of us could hear it. She clearly knew whether it was our car from the sound of the engine, even when the car was still a mile or more from home.

She would go anywhere with me, on or off the farm, often going well ahead if she thought she could predict where we were heading. When I was carrying my butterfly net, she would always head towards Smully Ham and the way up to the Reservoir. I estimated that her walks were about ten times as long as mine, because every bush and thicket had to be thoroughly investigated and she liked to include a wallow (or several) in the stream to cool off. If I shouted 'rabbits!' she became supercharged, tearing around with her nose to the ground. Rabbits were considered fair game as far as she was concerned, but she never chased a farm cat, chicken or duck.

All this crashing about in the undergrowth was not without its dangers. I often wondered how Lucy avoided getting thorns in her eyes and paws, or why she never seemed to get stung by nettles. She seemed to be impervious to such hazards. Then one day she came back limping. We returned to the house slowly as she was soon walking on three legs. I could still see nothing wrong with the foot other than that it had swollen to twice its normal size. Thinking that she had maybe broken a small bone in her foot, we took her to the vet. It turned out to be something quite different. She had been bitten by an adder. There were lots of adders on the farm and on occasion the cows got bitten on the nose or mouth. I ignored this danger. How would it be possible to chase butterflies if you were constantly worried about where you were putting your feet? Anyway, Lucy got injected with antiserum and recovered rapidly. A few days later she was charging around as if nothing had happened. My most notable encounter with adders was up on Bealey's Hill. This was an area of scrub on the opposite side of the valley to our farm, where on several occasions I saw two of these snakes, a brown and cream female and a black and silver male. They were the largest adders I had ever seen and had a favourite basking place in the sun. I assume they were a breeding pair. I was ultra-cautious when going up there to watch them.

Occasionally, as a treat, we were taken for a trip to the coast, which was only about seven miles away. We usually went to Westward Ho! This had a vast sandy beach where we could run around with Lucy, throwing sticks or balls. She had no fear of the waves and would retrieve objects from the sea. Very often there were flocks of seabirds, usually gulls, and Lucy shot off in their direction, knowing from experience that she had no hope of catching them. They would wait until she got close then lazily lift into the air and settle again further down the beach. Behind the pebble ridge were sand dunes, with more rabbits to chase. Visits to the coast nearly always came up with interesting finds, usually shells. However, on one occasion we found something quite extraordinary and unexpected at the side of a lane close to the sand dunes. It was an enormous African buffalo horn. I have no idea how it got there or to whom it might have belonged, but we took it home. It is still here beside me as I write.

We would often call in at one of the rocky coves further west along the coast, including Greencliff, Shipload Bay and Hartland Point. At Greencliff, after a storm, we found exciting objects down in the pools, such as a rope ladder with wooden steps and a lifebuoy with the words 'American Crusader, New York'. Much to Lucy's excitement we dragged these up the cliff paths and stuffed them into the car. Back at the farm we fixed the rope ladder up an oak tree close to the house and made a swing out of the lifebuoy. At Shipload Bay Lucy performed her Reservoir routine, flushing insects from the gorse bushes and bracken. There was a creamy coloured day-flying moth, the scarce blackneck, that was common there but found only in a few North Devon bays, nowhere else in Britain. This was quite a find but difficult to explain. Why had it not spread to neighbouring rocky bays that looked very similar? I have never found the answer to that question.

The concept of taking a dog for a walk did not apply to Lucy. I loved to roam the country, looking out for wildlife, and Lucy simply came wherever I went. One place I liked to go was about half a mile beyond the Reservoir, called Foxes Cross. This was an area of woodland that rang with bird song in spring and was carpeted in flowers. On one memorable day Lucy was taking an inordinate interest in a hole in the trunk of a half-dead tree, about two metres up. I thought I had better check it out. It looked the perfect place, I thought, in which some largish birds might nest but was more likely inhabited by squirrels. I scrambled up and peeped in. There, sitting a few inches from my face, was what looked like a fluffy toy with deep dark eyes. It was a well-grown tawny owl chick. This was quite a find, but after looking at it for a few minutes, I decided to retreat. Tawny owls can be rather aggressive when defending their nests. The tree was right next to the path, which was unusual as these are normally shy birds. I didn't want to make the adults desert their nest and was keen to pay it cautious visits over the next few weeks to see how it was doing. I also wanted to collect some of the regurgitated owl pellets from the ground beneath, so that I could compare their contents with those pellets from our barn owls in Old Blackaton. Complete skulls could be found in such pellets, and these could be compared and identified from photographs in books I possessed. In my bedroom I had a whole collection of such skulls, mainly from mice, voles, shrews but also the occasional bird.

On another visit to the woods, along the same path, Lucy and I came face to face with a fox, quietly walking towards us. I grabbed Lucy's collar in case she decided to give chase. The fox just watched us for a few minutes, then slunk into the undergrowth to the right of the path. Lucy and I followed with our eyes the shaking of leaves as the unseen fox pushed through the brambles. It did a big semi-circle around us and joined the path behind us. She then stood in full view, watching us for a few moments before carrying on along the path as if the encounter had never happened.

That day we had another strange encounter, but this one was a bit frightening. We walked on for a mile or so and came to a bank where trees had been felled a few years previously. The bank was covered in thick but low vegetation, about a metre high. Thinking this might be a good place for butterflies, we tramped around for a bit but found nothing unusual. I then came out onto a farm track and waited for Lucy to emerge. I couldn't see her directly but, as with the fox, tracked her progress by looking at the swaying vegetation. I then heard a slight scuffing sound and looked to my left. Standing on the path was a man with a shotgun, which he had trained on the place where Lucy was progressing. This was a potentially dangerous situation and I had to act immediately. I decided to call Lucy's name, loudly, then looked back to where the man had been standing. He had disappeared. More than a little spooked by this encounter and feeling a little shaky, I decided it was time for us to do the same thing and go home.

20

Lucy and the Pups

Every six months or so Lucy would come into season. She clearly had no idea why she was kept indoors and resented it. Who would be guarding the house? Who would be making sure that Tulip was not bothering the Guinea pigs? Would the farmyard cats be messing with her carefully hidden bones? The house was a busy place, with up to six people clattering round at the same time, and Lucy desperately needed to be out there in her usual place on top of the wall or helping me on our walks across the farm. She would try to squeeze out when anyone opened the back door but was either pushed back (inexplicably) or taken out briefly on the lead to relieve herself. There was clearly something interesting going on outside. Dogs were appearing from all the farms in the district, some from miles away. Occasionally there would be fights. This motley collection included sheep dogs (lots of these), Jack Russells, enormous crossbreeds and dogs of every other size, shape and colouring that you could imagine. It took two people to take Lucy outside, one to keep a firm hold on her lead and another with a stick to keep these dogs at bay.

Despite our precautions, it was almost impossible to keep the situation under control. People would visit the house who did not understand that we were in a state of siege. The inevitable happened. Lucy's belly started to enlarge, and it was clear that one or more of these dogs had had its wicked way with her. After nine weeks a litter of pups was born. All of them looked like sheep dogs and were black and white. We suspected one particularly persistent suitor, a large, old sheep dog with one eye (whom we christened One-Eyed Riley). We decided to keep two pups and asked the vet to put the rest to sleep. It was great fun having these two pups and they grew fast as all their mother's milk was available to them. Lucy was a good and dedicated mother. The pups were given away to neighbours at around eight weeks old.

A year later the whole thing was repeated. Lucy escaped again and this time clearly mated with an animal that looked like a fluffy husky. We kept one pup this time, a long-haired jet black dog. I would have loved to have kept it but again it was given away to people we trusted to look after it well.

Another six months passed and this time we managed to fight off the suitors successfully. Rearing pups is a messy business, and rearing mongrels that had to be given away was not a very sensible strategy. The farm had to make money and Lucy should play her part. So, much to my glee, it was decided that she should be mated to a pedigree golden retriever dog. Now it so happened that the place where we stayed overnight on our arrival in Devon, the Black Horse in the Torrington town square, had exactly what we were looking for. This dog was huge, pale cream and with a lovely temperament. He could be seen on most days lying in the road outside his home, fully expecting the traffic to go round him. The town children loved him and gave him titbits, which probably contributed to his size. A price was agreed for his services and the deed was done.

As she approached her due date, Lucy grew enormous. It looked likely that she was going to produce more pups than she had from her previous pregnancies. She started building dens in what she considered to be good locations, such as thick hedges. The one where she spent the most time was under the floor of the little summer house by the tennis court. There was barely room for her to squeeze into this dusty hollow. She did some nest building involving a lot of digging, which may have deepened the hollow but also managed to get her completely covered with fine soil. She was quite happy to shake it off when she was back in the farm-house. One evening she refused to come back to the house, so we left her there overnight. The next morning there was a chorus of mewlings and squeaks, the unmistakable sounds of new-born puppies.

Now it is very easy for a bitch with new-born pups in a confined space to squash one or two by accident. The whole family had to be moved, but we were worried that wherever we took them Lucy would want to bring them back. In fact, that didn't happen. With great difficulty we had to crawl under the summer house and pass the pups out one at a time. Lucy watched this process with an anxious frown but did not interfere. Then they were carried in a basket into the house, where we had made a soft bed of old blankets in a cupboard next to the Ideal Cook 'n Heat. Lucy took to this immediately and to calm the pups down fed them. After the exertions of the night, involving giving birth to a massive twelve puppies, she fell asleep.

The pups were simply gorgeous. They ranged from the pale cream of the father through to deep gold of Lucy. We liked to get into the cupboard with the pups and have them crawling all over us. Lucy started to lose a lot of weight, depleted by her huge family, so we started to give supplementary food to the pups from an early age. Now cow's milk is not ideal for puppies, but we had a never-ending supply of it, so that's what they got. They grew like golden mushrooms. I vividly remember Mum taking them out onto Hodge's Down when they were old enough and rolling around in the grass with pups climbing all over her. They liked to lick your face, stick their tongues in your ears and attack your clothing, especially shoelaces. When they moved together, they were like a flock of small, fat, golden seal pups, with black eyes and noses. If I had had my way, we would have kept them all. By the time they were old enough to be sold Lucy was completely exhausted and seemed glad to see the back of them. Mum was similarly affected. Keeping such a boisterous bunch fed and clean was a marathon task.

We did in fact keep one, Burt. He grew into a large, pale and handsome dog. Unfortunately, he came to a sad end. Nobody had time to train him properly, with disastrous results. The first indication that something was wrong was when I discovered the chewed up remains of several geese and chickens on the old tennis court.

We tried to teach him that killing poultry was against the rules but to no avail. I don't think he was particularly bright. We worried that he might turn to killing cats or our neighbours' sheep. We couldn't pass on a dog with such behaviour to anyone else and so sadly we had to have him put down. It upset me badly.

21
The Great Winter of 1962-63

We had been on the farm for two years when the Great Winter struck, with very little warning. At first small amounts of snow fell, and it was all great fun. The sun shone on the lines of snow coating every twig and leaf, and the fields were covered with arctic whiteness. We expected it all to melt away, as was usually the case in Devon, but the opposite happened. It started snowing again, heavily, and went on for days. Huge flakes came down so thickly you could not see far. Strong winds blew it into drifts, and the roads became blocked. The temperature dropped as low as -14°F (-25°C). Justin was ecstatic; he had never recorded temperatures anywhere near as low as this before. Drifts of snow formed, reportedly up to 6 metres high, blown by winds of up to 80mph. It was the coldest weather recorded since 1740. For the farmers this was a major disaster, and it could easily have destroyed us.

Of immediate concern were the cows. Each stall had a drinker, operated by the cows' noses, and all of them froze up. Normally you wouldn't expect this to happen as the cowshed was always warm in winter, kept so by the heat from the cows. None of the pipes were lagged to prevent freezing. The only source of water was the stream, which itself was frozen over. The ice had to be broken up with pickaxes and the shallow water scooped into milk churns and dragged up the steep bank from the stream into the farmyard. The churns were far too heavy for me to help with this task, which had to take place throughout the day for many days. The cows then had to be let out in small groups so that they could walk over to plastic tanks of stream water set up in the yard. They were cautious at first, not at all familiar with this strange whiteness covering the yard, but then became frisky, kicking their heels up and having mock battles with each other.

We had no mains electricity on the farm at this stage, and power was provided by a generator. This started to struggle under the cold conditions, and we had to use a small back-up generator in the dairy. Milking was therefore possible, fortunately, but with all the roads for miles around blocked by snow drifts the milk lorry could not get through. All the milk for many days had to be tipped into the stream and was wasted. The financial loss was considerable.

Every job was made harder. Simply getting bales of hay across the yard to the cowshed was a struggle. The snow was deep in the yard, much of it blown down from Hodges Down above. Cleaning out the muck from the cowshed was equally difficult, trying to push heavy wheelbarrows through the thick snow was no joke. Even the farm cats had difficulty picking their way along tractor wheel marks to get to the cowshed, morning and evening, to be given their milk. All the farm cats had white fur but looked rather grubby against the pure white of the snow.

All the water pipes in the house froze up, too. When possible, the pipes were thawed out with rags soaked in hot water, but the problem with that was that they had burst in many places by the expansion of the ice and leaked everywhere when the thaw came. Dad was able to temporarily bind up the leaks with insulating tape, then tied them tightly with bailer twine. Keeping a supply of water going for the kitchen, bathroom and toilet was very difficult. We all got both very cold and exhausted, not to mention filthy. We became marooned for many days by ice and snow, nobody could get in or out of the farm.

There was a limited number of jobs with which my brothers and I could help, and we did. However, I took every opportunity I could to explore this white landscape. In many places the snow was blown into frozen waves, much like large sea waves beloved by surfers in places like Hawaii or those in Japanese paintings. Everything was frozen in place by the extreme cold. You could actually walk or crawl along inside these waves, especially where they had formed over a hedge. I managed to work my way up to the Reservoir with some difficulty and found it to be completely frozen over. I kicked a few stones free from the ground and sent them skipping over the ice. The noise they made is hard to describe but was like the sounds of hollow sticks being struck together. Very foolishly I tried walking out on the ice. After a few metres the ice started to crack and subsided a few centimetres without breaking up. I found it very difficult to get back to the bank as the ice was now sloping slightly causing me to slip backwards, away from the bank. I was mightily relieved to get out. I think it was one of the most stupid things I have ever done and still get shivers down my spine when I think about it.

The snow on Hodges Down was blown into deep drifts. At the top of the field, we rolled the snow into large snowballs and then let gravity do the rest. Given a good push to start them off, they rolled down the field, getting faster and bigger as they went. Some broke up as they galloped down the field, others managed to reach the bottom by which time they were enormous, far taller than we were. They were stopped by the hedge between Hodges Down and Upper Newpark. It was difficult to 'aim' the snowball as they were quite likely to veer off course on their way down. Unfortunately, one of mine managed to hit the double gates at the bottom and burst them open. I am amazed they weren't shattered, although the gate catch was bent. Apart from going down and shutting the gates, I kept quiet about this inadvertent misdemeanour and fortunately got away with it. One of these huge snowballs managed to stop outside the back of our house and was made into a giant and very fat snowman. It looked a bit odd though, with a disproportionately small head and huge body. The head was made with the largest snowball that it was possible for us to lift into place.

22

White Cats

It is normal practice when a farm is sold for the cats to be part of the deal. These farm cats never come into the house; their sole duty is to catch rats, mice and rabbits. This is sensible because cats brought up together will get on OK and know their way around. They know where to go in spring to catch young bunnies and where the best places were to ambush rats and mice. All the cats that came with our farm were pure white, which is unusual. We decided to keep this tradition going. They were beautiful ethereal animals in their own right. You would think that their lack of camouflage would make them poor mousers, but that did not seem to be the case. They had a pretty good life. In exchange for their hard work, they could eat all the small rodents they could find, get fed as much milk as they wanted at milking times and the rest of the day they could spend sleeping in the hay. I envied them this somewhat hedonistic lifestyle.

All farms need to keep their cat numbers in check, or they would soon be overrun. The only problem with keeping white cats exclusively was that there were frequent visits by multi-coloured toms. These scabby-looking cats have a hard life because they have to fight for mating rights against any resident toms. And, of course, they were not white. From time to time clusters of kittens were born, usually in amongst the hay bales, and any that were not white were put to sleep by the vet. We did make an exception to this rule once, and that was for a white cat with a pure black tail. Any visiting toms (if they could be caught they were very wild) were put down and some of the white males castrated. We aimed to keep the numbers below ten. This may seem harsh, but it was not very different from selectively breeding farm animals such as cows. In addition, everything was done humanely on our farm, which was not always the case elsewhere.

Farm cats are usually smaller than house cats, probably because they are not fed on carefully formulated cat foods. This was demonstrated clearly when we gave a white kitten to my aunt Lina in Cheltenham. Fed well and cossetted, it grew into one of the biggest cats I have ever seen. Like the golden retriever dog from the Black Horse, this cat (called Willow) used to lie in the road, expecting the traffic to go around it. In this instance it was clear that being conspicuous (rather than camouflaged) was a good survival strategy.

There was a curious genetic problem with our white cats. A small proportion were born with one yellow eye and the other a bright blue, like the eye of a Siamese cat. These odd-eyed cats were always deaf. In other respects, they were perfectly healthy but unfortunately did not live long. With regular movements by farm machinery and delivery vehicles, these cats just did not hear or respond to approaching wheels until it was too late. Sometimes kittens would be stepped on by the cows.

The farm cats received a much-appreciated supplement to their diets whenever I went fishing. The Parnells, the previous owners of the farm, moved to St Giles in the Wood where they had several fishing lakes. This was only a few miles away, and I would cycle over there on my rickety old bike, taking my fishing gear and a bag to carry my catch home. These lakes were, I believe, originally constructed to feed into a canal that ran along the valley of the River Torridge (long since disappeared). I had an open invitation to fish in these lakes, in part because the Parnells knew that some of what I caught would go to the cats. I was therefore encouraged to take away anything I managed to catch. In theory removing smaller fish, such as rudd and perch, would result in a mean increase in the size of the fish that remained. I didn't have a fishing rod and simply used a stick to which some line was tied with a hook on it. On one such expedition I managed to catch over fifty fish. They were far too small and bony to cook, but the cats loved them raw. When I dropped a few in the farmyard, each cat would squabble like crazy over them then grab one and run off, growling, to eat it in peace. They would then come back for another. Eventually, when all the fish were gone, the cats waddled off with fat bellies to digest this glorious meal in the hay barn. I tried offering one of these fish to Tulip but he rejected it with the deepest contempt.

Occasionally the farm cats received trout, not from the Parnell's lakes I hasten to add but from the stream running through our farm. These were fish that had escaped from the Reservoir by swimming through the outflow pipe. They could be found in the deeper pools but were very wary, and conventional fishing techniques would not work. Instead, I used an old poaching technique for catching fish. I found a long stick, fixed a staple into the end and made a noose out of fishing line. I very slowly dipped the end of the stick with its noose into the water upstream of the trout and let it drift down with the current. The noose slipped over the head of the trout without disturbing it, and with a quick pull on the line I could catch it behind the gills and pull it onto the bank. I only did this for fish large enough to be worth eating. They were delicious. The cats got the heads.

The relationship between the white farm cats and Tulip was interesting. The farm cats never came down to the house and I never saw Tulip in the farmyard. Somehow, he exerted his dominance, which was total. I do not remember any fights; they did not seem to be necessary. How a neutered tabby cat, brought up in suburbia, could intimidate a rough bunch of farm cats and keep them out of his territory is a mystery. Judging by the number of torn ears, the farm cats had no compunction about fighting amongst themselves.

23
Wild Birds

The word 'manicured' sums up precisely what our farm certainly was not. There were lots of boggy corners, areas with impenetrable gorse and bramble thickets. The hedgerows were broad, spilling into the surrounding fields, and were rarely cut. Indeed, the only hedges that were cut every year were those bordering the Old Barnstaple Road. Thus, the farm was a haven for wildlife of every kind. Dad believed that all this mixed vegetation was good for the health of the cows, who liked to browse on it even when there was plenty of grass available. The boggy areas were thick with thistles, some taller than myself, that were in turn densely covered in pollinating insects, especially bees, hoverflies, moths and butterflies.

As a result, birdlife flourished, including ground-nesting birds that even then were declining because of changes in farming methods. We had, for example, both quail and grey partridges, plus nests of larks. In the broad and bushy hedgerows were yellowhammers, with their lovely little-bit-of-bread-and-no-cheese song. Even in the farmyard the buildings were full of swallow and house sparrow nests, not to mention the bats that made high-pitched buzzing sounds, which we boys could hear but Mum and Dad could not. In winter huge flocks of murmurating starlings would darken the sky and take minutes to pass over, wheeling through the air like massive shoals of fish. Similarly, there were great flocks of twittering finches, intermittently coming to earth to feed on the weed seeds or grain left over from barley crops. For some reason they induced me to sing, at the top of my voice, 'Birds of the air I adore you, you whistle and sing to me' to the tune of the Eton Boating Song. There was real joy in watching the extraordinary patterns that the flocks made in the sky.

One day a very strange bird turned up. I was walking along Smully Ham when out of the shrubbery flanking the stream came a musical gonging sound. It was unlike anything I had heard before. After much scrambling around I managed to spot it. The bird was about the size of a starling and mossy green in colour. This did not fit with any British bird, and I realised immediately that it must be an escapee. Later, on a visit to Paignton Zoo, I was able to tentatively identify it as a New Zealand bellbird. Possibly it was someone's escaped pet, or it might have come from the small zoo in Bideford that had been recently established. However, from then on it was referred to as the Gong Gong bird. Although I made several visits to Smully Ham over the next few days, I never saw nor heard it calling again.

We knew that there were sometimes people shooting ducks on the Reservoir, and Justin and I foolishly decided to try to do something about it. The shooting took place at dusk, when the ducks would come in to spend the night in (they thought) safety in the middle of the lake. So just before dusk we crept up to the Reservoir and hid up at the far end where there was a good view over the water and plenty of cover. Our aim was to shout and wave our arms around to persuade the ducks not to land. Suddenly, when it was getting quite dark, a man with a shotgun loomed up behind us. He was not pleased. He ordered us angrily to go away, which we did. Arguing with a man carrying a shotgun did not seem wise. I suspect he was angry partly because he might well have shot us by mistake if we had been hiding anywhere else, or he had come down to the Reservoir from a different direction. He was right, we were foolish, but in all the kerfuffle we may have achieved our objective, at least for that night. I was annoyed by the duck hunting in part because a few days prior to this I had found a dead little grebe in the water that had clearly been shot. There was no excuse for shooting a grebe, which is clearly not a game bird.

I had no objection to hunters who wished to come onto our farm to shoot pheasants, wood pigeons and rabbits, and indeed Dad encouraged them to do so. After a day's shooting they shared their bag with us, and Mum would (somewhat reluctantly) prepare and cook them. They tasted good, especially the rabbits, but sorting out the shot from the meat was unpleasant.

The wild bird that had the greatest effect on me was a magpie called Marius. I had long planned his arrival by breeding up my white mouse colony to provide lots of babies to feed to him. This was a substitute for a major part of the diet of wild magpies, namely songbird chicks. I had wanted a magpie for some time after reading about the mischievous pair kept by Gerald Durrell in Corfu and described in *My Family and Other Animals*. I knew exactly where to find him – in the nest on the Christmas Tree Patch. I had to be achingly patient, watching the magpies refurbish their nest for another season, recording the laying of eggs and predicting when they would hatch. The eggs were an exquisite bluish colour, speckled all over with greenish spots. I kept an eye on developments using a mirror on the end of a stick. Eventually they hatched and I decided to collect one at a week old. This was old enough to be robust but also young enough for it to imprint on me as a surrogate parent.

The nest was well defended. Firstly, the tree holding the nest was thorny and I got horribly prickled. Once I had reached the nest, I then had to find the nest entry point which was by no means simple. The birds do an excellent job of hiding it. I didn't want to force my way into their prickly globe for fear they might desert. Taking one of their offspring was bad enough, destroying their nest and the remaining chicks would be unforgivable. I took a strong-looking chick, put it inside my shirt and managed to get down the tree without squashing it against the thorny branches.

The chick looked like a tiny vulture suffering from alopecia. I had everything ready for his (or her, I have no idea which) arrival. In my bedroom I kept a rather smelly terrapin in a small fish tank, containing a couple of inches of water and a rock. The water temperature was kept high using a normal fish tank heater. The terrapin and Marius had to share the tank. I had prepared a tin, previously contained cocoa powder, by adding some small pieces of rag. Marius sat on top of this, and I let the whole thing set sail in the warm water.

For food he mostly had a mix of baby mice, hard boiled hen's eggs and any invertebrates I could find (slugs, woodlice, pupae, caterpillars, etc.). I also added some commercial 'egg biscuit' food that I used for a range of birds as a rearing supplement. He grew fast and his tin had to be wedged in a corner of the tank to stop it falling over. Soon he was spending most of his time perched on the side of the tank. As a young chick I just kept stuffing his red gape with food until he had had enough. Once he was older, he snatched pieces of food from a pair of forceps, then learnt to peck up his food from a bowl.

He rapidly developed black and white feathers but looked pretty rumpled, like someone who has forgotten to do the ironing. At this stage, before he learnt to fly, I would carry him around on my shoulder to get him used to the idea. He watched everything carefully but was a bold bird and hadn't learnt to be afraid of anything. Lucy and Tulip were told in no uncertain terms that this bird was off limits. I even took him along on one of our visits to the coast. We walked through the sand dunes, getting surprised comments from visitors who either cringed away from him, fearful that he would try to peck them, or who wanted to stroke him. Either way, he seemed to like the attention. Often on walks I would catch a beetle or spider and offer it to him as a snack, which he accepted gracefully.

Marius by this time lived in his own aviary behind the house. He was very fussy about who fed him and only fully accepted me if I was wearing a particular jacket. A time came when I had to go away for a couple of weeks (hitch-hiking around Ireland) and I left him in the hands of my parents. While I was away Dad decided that the aviary needed an extra perch and so made a hole in the netting on each side of the run and put a branch through the holes. This probably worked well for a time, but the pressure of the bird landing on the branch gradually made the holes from which it was suspended larger. One day Marius squeezed out and was never seen again. I hope that if I had been there, wearing the right jacket, he would have stayed around looking for me. That is possibly what he did for a while. It was very sad to lose him. Hopefully he taught himself how to find his own food in the wild.

24

Private School

Having failed the 11-Plus exam I could not go to the Grammar School in Bideford and was sent instead to Belmont College, a private school in Barnstaple. The two years I spent there were the worst years of my life. It was run mainly by ex-army men who had no idea about how to teach but had devised some inventive ways of imposing discipline and planning punishments. The idea was to force boys to learn through fear. For example, the Latin master, Colonel Yule, would set us some Latin vocabulary to learn overnight then come to the class next day swinging a cane. He would periodically whack this down on a desk. If you got the translation of two words wrong, you were caned in front of the class. At the end of that year my Latin exam mark was second highest in the class, with a score of seventeen per cent. In French it was no better. This was taken by the Headmaster, Colonel Oldfield. He decided that our French exams results were so poor that we all had to repeat the whole year. For Maths we had a Mr Parrot. He came to class apparently without a cane. However, if he thought someone was being cheeky, he would pull a cane out of his trousers and beat the boy concerned in front of the whole class. Strangely I always thought of Maths as my worst subject, but in the exam I came first. I received as a prize, a copy of *Three Men in a Boat*, which I can recommend to anyone.

Most of the other masters were just as bad. For a particularly serious misdemeanour, the punishment would be conducted in a ritualistic manner. The whole school was turned out to watch the guilty boy being marched across from the main building (an old manor house) to the gymnasium. He would be followed by Colonel Oldfield, swishing around a massive cane, plus other members of staff. We then had to listen to the crack of the cane and the cries of the boy. It seemed to go on forever.

On one day I arrived at school and saw an ambulance near the front of the building and a body lying on a stretcher. A new teacher, who had been tormented by the older boys, had tried to kill himself by cutting his wrists and jumping from a window. I don't know for certain whether he survived, we were not told, but the word was that he had died.

For two years I lived in extreme fear. The boys turned on each other too, like wolves picking on any show of weakness. There was a chapel where we had morning assembly. We boys arrived there before the staff. The older boys set a look-out, then proceeded to beat up their chosen victim before the staff arrived. These were severe beatings, and they would often beat up the same boy, daily, for weeks on end. They liked to have a victim that would fight back rather than one who just cowered in terror.

I had a problem of a related nature, although not to quite the same degree. To get to school I had to cycle down from the farm to the railway station each day, whatever the weather. I then caught the steam train to Barnstaple along with four other Belmont pupils. Everything went OK for several months, but then one boy, egged on by the rest, tried to goad me into a fight. Fighting has never been in my nature and so I tried to ignore it. This boy started to rub soot into my face to try and induce a reaction. I put up with this for a couple of days but eventually broke. As we were about to get off the train one evening, I punched him as hard as I could in the face. Just a single punch. Apparently, I knocked a couple of his teeth loose and was warned that his father would be coming after me. Fortunately, nothing happened. If the headmaster had heard about it, I would probably have had to take that walk of shame between the schoolhouse and the gym.

To avoid further trouble, Mum managed to find someone, Mr Cox, one of our neighbours, who would give me a lift to and from Barnstaple where he worked in a garage. In the evening I left school some time before he left work, and instead of waiting for him at the Old Barnstaple Road I would walk down to his garage in town. I was accompanied by Nigel, a good friend from school who had a great interest in wildlife too. We walked through an area of scrubby wasteland, spoilt somewhat by industrial rubbish but with interesting insects. In particular there were clusters of colourful Lackey moth larvae, with blue and red stripes, that fed colonially on the bushes.

Nigel and I went camping on Exmoor once, which was great fun. We camped near the Doon Valley, surrounded by wonderful hillsides covered in a brilliant patchwork of yellow (gorse) and red (heather) scrub. We cooked our evening meals over an open fire. When the sky was clear of clouds you could see billions of stars. At school Nigel was a much-needed ally. He had a particular interest in reptiles, including common lizards caught on the moors, and even managed to breed them by feeding the youngsters on aphids and other tiny insects.

I could tell many unpleasant stories about Belmont College but would rather not dwell on it. I am told that the place was closed down not so long after I left. Despite learning practically nothing during the time I was there, I managed to pass my 13-plus exam somehow and escaped from their clutches. I moved to Bideford Grammar School, which was a much more enlightened place, but do wonder what would have become of me if I had had to remain at Belmont for several more years. My intense fear of school never quite went away.

25

Cows with Bad Habits

I can see that the concept of running a 'flying herd' makes a lot of sense, on paper. You avoid the labour and expense of rearing replacements. You maximise the number of milking cows that your land could hold. All your efforts can be concentrated upon growing the lushest, most productive crops of grass, maximising the amount of milk you get, from grass per cow. What you miss, however, is the opportunity to breed replacement from your most high-yielding animals. Replacement cows that are bought in from markets and farm sales are of completely unknown provenance. If ever I got the chance to run a dairy farm, I would get far more satisfaction from it if I could institute a strict breeding programme and only rear the best of the best.

We ourselves would sell off cows that were unproductive, difficult to get in calf, had medical problems or were simply badly behaved. The worst place to buy cows was at the markets where we and others sold their misfits while the best place was farm sales. At the latter all cows would be sold off, not just the troublesome ones, and buyers were usually given a schedule detailing each cow's history, including the number of calves it has had and when. Cattle dealers were another option. We bought many Ayrshire cows from a dealer who would buy these at farm sales in Scotland and ship them down to us. They were a little more expensive but saved you the trouble of going to sales yourself.

Dad did buy cows from markets sometimes, and so it was not very surprising that we managed to buy several cows that had behavioural problems, some rather amusing. First there were the kickers. These were often first calvers, not used to being milked, who simply tried to kick the machine off as you were trying to put it on. In bad cases a rope tied tightly around the withers solved this problem. In time they lost this habit and became used to the system. We had a couple of cows who accepted the milking machine but would kick off the cluster when they thought that most of the milk had been taken and we were not being quick enough at removing it. This was annoying as the cluster would often get covered in muck and had to be cleaned. Another cow found the process of washing her teats prior to attaching the cluster unbearably ticklish. She didn't kick but instead hunched herself up, paddling her back hooves up and down, making attachment of the cluster very difficult. Once it was on, she was as good as gold. I think she found the washing of her teats unbearably tickly. There were two cows that caused problems in the field when we were operating an electric fence that was moved every day to provide fresh strips of grass or in the winter kale. One cow would attempt to jump over the fence but wasn't quite as athletic as she thought. Invariably she caught the fence with one of her back hooves, pulling the whole thing down. Suddenly all of this luscious forage was available to the whole herd, and they made the most of it. You could not help wondering whether this was all planned in advance, with several senior cows egging on this high jumper. The other cow did the opposite. She would push under the fence, apparently unaffected by the pulses of electricity passing through the wire and thus into her back. This would pull the fence posts out of the ground, and again the whole heard rejoiced and invaded the rest of the field. Both cows were sold at market when they next calved. I suspect that over the years these two animals were bought and sold many times by a string of disgruntled dairy farmers.

Many of the cows we bought in had recently calved. They looked impressive in the market, with their bulging udders and squirting teats (achieved by omitting the morning milking). In practice some of them then proved very difficult to get in calf. Possibly this would have been less of a problem if we kept our own bull rather than using artificial insemination. If the herd had been bigger (we had up to fifty cows at any one time), a bull might have been justified, although handling bulls comes with its own problems.

Another problem with constantly buying in replacement cows is that it upsets the hierarchy within the herd. The new animal had to fight its way up through this hierarchy until it reached its rightful place in the pecking order. This disrupted the whole herd and adversely affected milk production for a few days.

26

The Christmas Tree Patch

A favourite wildlife area for me on the farm was the Christmas Tree Patch. This was a fenced-off, rather boggy area at the bottom of Higher Hodges, half of which was planted with young Christmas trees. The rest of the area was a mass of sallow and brambles. It was stiff with rabbits, which emerged into the surrounding fields at dusk. For the first few years we harvested some of the Christmas trees and sold them to a greengrocer in Torrington. We didn't replant, and as a result the whole site was left to its own devices. It did, of course, mean that we could choose the best Christmas tree for ourselves and thus always had a magnificent specimen. Eventually I asked Dad if I could have this piece of land and do with it whatever I chose; he agreed.

My aim was to turn it into an area even more suitable for wildlife. Therefore, the first thing I did was to fell some larger pine trees, the remains of an earlier planting of Christmas trees. This opened up an area that previously had little light and hence no understory of plants. I felt like an early pioneer, harvesting timber for log fires. There was already a lot of bird life (including the magpie's nest), and the place was great for moths (the larvae of many species of moth feed on sallow). I would come along at dusk with my net and catch whatever I could find without snaring the net on the brambles. I also painted a mix of sugar, molasses and alcohol onto the tree trunks, which attracted a different set of species to those lured by a moth lamp. Caterpillars could be easily found by spreading a sheet beneath a branch and then beating the latter with a stick. By the height of summer, my bedroom was full of jars containing different species which I attempted to rear through to adults. The species I particularly treasured were caterpillars of the elephant, poplar and eyed hawkmoths with their dramatic horn on their rear ends.

The brambles provided us with excellent crops of blackberries, which Mum turned into blackberry and apple pies, blackberry crumbles and blackberry jam. Brambles have both flowers and fruit at the same time and in particular rotting fruit attracted a lot of butterflies and other insects. These included bees, hoverflies, ladybirds, spittle bugs, social wasps and parasitic wasps, along with a whole community of different species of spiders. To me this mix was glorious, to the rest of the family it was of no interest whatsoever.

27

Donkeys

On our journey down to the farm I had speculated on the remote possibility of getting a horse one day. I had fantasies about travelling across Dartmoor on this horse, camping each night in a tent and looking for moorland wildlife by day. I nearly got my wish, but in the form of a donkey, Antigua. This donkey came from a breeding herd and had been running with a pure white jack. There was the possibility, therefore, that Antigua was pregnant and that her foal could be white. After two years of eager anticipation, I had to accept the fact that this was not, unfortunately, going to happen. Nevertheless, Antigua was a beautiful donkey who lived in the lower orchard, adjoining the tennis court. I thought maybe travelling across the moors with her might still be possible, but I would have to walk while she carried the baggage (tent, food and entomological equipment). Antigua had other ideas, or least she had one idea and that was, at all costs, not to cooperate. She would not accept being led on a halter; the only way I could get her to go in the direction I wanted was to walk in front of her holding a bucket of her favourite concentrates. This was not a practical method for crossing the moors. Perhaps I would have been better to have tried Susie-two as my pack animal, at least she was trained to accept a halter. I might have attracted some very strange looks, especially from farmers who would not have liked to see a full-grown cow being led across their land.

I rather hoped that maybe we could take Antigua to meet a jack and use her as a breeding animal, but that never came to pass. We decided to give her some company. In those days the main function of donkeys seemed to be to give children rides on the beach during the summer. These beach donkeys had a hard life.

Over the winter they were found willing homes, and we decided to offer such a home to this animal, called Jenny. She was a thick-set, stolid animal who seemed to be lost in her own thoughts most of the time.

28

Sticks and the Zoo

A widely held misconception by non-farming people is that a herds-man carries a stick in order to whack the cows. This is completely wrong. If you tried hitting a donkey with a stick, the animal would probably just look at you sorrowfully and carry on with whatever it was doing, usually nothing. Cows on the other hand knew exactly what was being asked of them and usually cooperated. When bring-ing in the cows for milking, you would use the stick to lightly tap the animals bringing up the rear just to remind them that you were still there and that they needed to keep up with the rest of the herd. You could guide the direction in which they were going by touching them on the side. Mostly you just waved the stick around without touching them at all. It is an effective means of communication between herdsman and cows. The stick acted as an extension to your arm in case they were thinking about turning back or loitering over a particularly tasty bit of foliage in a hedgerow. True, under certain circumstance a harder tap may be necessary, for example when a cow was bulling (coming into season and jumping on each other's backs). At such times they were so distracted that they might otherwise blunder into you. At other times they may be defending a new-born calf and need reminding that you were the top cow in the herd, that there was nothing to worry about and they needed to calm down.

At one time I was able to get a summer holiday job at the new zoo that was being set up in Bideford. Amongst the more usual zoo animals, such as llamas, monkeys and a bear, was a beautiful Jersey cow. One day she escaped from her small enclosure and headed into the surrounding woods. There were four of us who set off to bring her back. All was going well until the zoo's owner came to help us. I was using a stick to show the cow which way we wanted her to go, and she was cooperating. The owner, Mrs Tottenham, started shouting at me, telling me to drop the stick and that if I wanted to thrash a cow I could go home and do that, but I was not allowed to treat her cow in such a cruel way.

I am sure this lady had her heart in the right place, but she had no idea how to communicate effectively with animals, or people. The number of animals that died during the short time I spent there was horrifying, mostly goats and monkeys. There was a chimpanzee in a tiny cage in which it could barely turn around. The poor animal tried to grab you as you went past, and I have had nightmares about this ever since. It had nothing to play with and no other animals for company and was not-so-quietly going mad. There was a red deer stag that seemed to spend the whole day charging the wire netting around its enclosure. To be fair, there were two things I really liked in that zoo. The first was a brown bear who would jump up against the bars of its cage to allow me to feed it bottles of milk and blood through the bars. It never tried to harm me in any way. Then there was a stable in which the whole floor was covered in a moving carpet of multi-coloured Guinea pigs. This could not fail to appeal to me.

I understand that the zoo only lasted for a few years.

29

The Aviaries

It started with Dad and *Doctor Who*. Dad used to tell me about how he had kept budgerigars as a teenager. The idea appealed to me greatly, but there was a significant problem and that was the cost of an aviary in which to keep the birds. However, for reasons explained elsewhere, I managed to pass my 13-plus exams and got into Bideford Grammar School. With extraordinary generosity Dad agreed to buy an aviary for me as a present to celebrate the passing of my exams. It arrived in a small lorry, right in the middle of the very first episode of *Doctor Who* on TV. I had had a glimpse of what this revolutionary science fiction serial was about in TV trailers and had been eagerly anticipating watching it for weeks. Logic suggested that the aviary could wait, it would still be there when the episode finished. *Doctor Who* could not wait (there was no way to record programmes in those days). So, I watched the rest of the programme and then rushed out to greet my new aviary enthusiastically. I know I had hurt Dad's feelings. On the other hand, he was probably delighted not to have to pay any further fees for my 'education' at the World's worst private school.

The purpose-built aviary consisted of a small shed, where the birds could shelter and be fed, and a long flight area. I fitted several nest boxes and then gradually accumulated some budgerigars, deciding to concentrate on birds that were various shades of blue, plus some albinos and lutinos. Green budgies were banned. The one problem was that I had no control of which male mated with which female, and even with self-chosen mated pairs there may have been some extra-pair mating going on. Budgies that are a mix of yellow, green and blue just look a mess.

The budgerigars were great fun to breed. If there were too many eggs or young chicks in one box, I could move a few around to other nest boxes to equalise the workload for the parents. I bought one female bird in a pet shop that was clearly an Australian pied, a strain of budges noted for their large size. This one was a cinnamon and white bird of great beauty. However, I soon discovered that pet shops are a bit like cattle markets; they are a good place to get rid of troublesome stock. She laid lots of eggs but killed her offspring shortly after they hatched, deliberately or through neglect. I therefore fostered any eggs that she laid with other budgie pairs. This worked well and the chicks grew into magnificent blue and white Australian pied-type birds.

Occasionally a budgerigar would escape. This was usually when I had to open the door to get into the run. It was exhilarating to watch them rocketing through the sky in a flash of blue. They are extraordinarily powerful flyers, calling loudly and joyfully as they swooped around like strangely colourful birds of prey. They looked decidedly wrong sitting in an apple tree. The usual pattern was that the bird would disappear completely for 24 hours, then return on the second day, probably because it was getting hungry or trying to find its mate or in some cases its nest box. The calls of the birds still in the aviary would have made it easy for the budgerigars to find their way home, possibly from as much as a mile away. They would settle on the wire netting, trying to get back into the aviary, and I managed to catch them there with my butterfly net.

At this point I read about keeping Liberty budgerigars or 'homing' budgerigars. This is a system in which the birds come back for food or to their broods in nest boxes but for the rest of the day fly free. For security they can be shut up at night. I wanted to try this and constructed the lobster-pot-type of arrangement that allowed the birds to enter the aviary easily at dusk but then find it difficult to find their way out again. Unfortunately, I never got to try it out. There were several very large laburnums in our garden. All parts of these trees are poisonous and can kill birds. I appealed to Dad to let me cut them down, but he would not give in. I admit that laburnums do look pretty in the spring, but nothing like as beautiful as my vision of a flock of free-flying budgerigars.

My collection of birds grew and grew. At one time or another I kept, and in many cases bred, Java sparrows, zebra finches, Harz Mountain roller canaries, cockatiels, weavers, redpolls, green singing finches, budgerigars and Bengalese finches. Of these, two species gave me the greatest pleasure, the weavers and the Java sparrows. I had a pair of what were advertised as 'half-masked weavers', but I am not sure that this was correct. The female died of unknown causes soon after I bought them, which was a pity; I would have loved to breed them. The males are dramatic birds, mostly bright yellow but with a black face. I gave him a bunch of coarse grass every day, and he wove it into complex baskets, mostly globular but with a woven tube curling up from the base, very much like a pitcher plant. These nests were works of considerable craftsmanship. He would attach the nest at the start of the process to the end of a single twig. He made several such nests in different parts of the aviary, as high as possible. The elaborate design had two primary objectives. One was to attract females (there weren't any, but he didn't know that). The females don't make nests but do know well-made ones when they see them and hence detect the presence of a fit male in the vicinity. The second reason was to make it difficult if not impossible for snakes to find their way in. There were snakes around, grass snakes and adders, but I didn't see any in the aviaries.

I had a specific plan for the Java sparrows. They are wonderful little birds, with a black head, white cheeks and a massive bright pink bill, a soft grey colour on the back and breast, a pinkish belly and a black tail. They look like miniature puffins. When I kept them there were two options: domestic versions that were either white or pied and kept as cage birds in S. E. Asia or the wild type, which are far more beautiful. The white birds have been bred in captivity for centuries and are easy to breed, but the 'normal' birds are caught in the wild and can only be bred with difficulty. My plan was to cross the two types, domestic and wild, then breed back to the wild plumage, creating a strain that had the beauty of the wild type combined with ease of breeding of the domestic birds. This plan worked well, but only for the three years that I kept them; more years were needed to get rid of the pied patches entirely. I wrote an article about this experiment for *Cage and Aviary Birds* magazine, which they published and paid me ten shillings (50 p). My first publication!

The problem with keeping animals is that they are very good at finding inventive ways of dying. The worst episode for me concerned the aviaries in the old generator room. At the time disaster struck, there was a mix of birds in these aviaries, including budgies, zebra finches, Bengalese finches and canaries, all at various stages of breeding. One morning I went in to feed them as usual before going to school. Usually as I approached the room, I would be greeted by a chorus of beautiful song, from the warbling of the canaries to the harsh, chattery notes of the budgies. This particular morning there was an eerie silence. I opened the door and found a scene more appropriate to a horror movie. The floor was littered with half-eaten, dead birds. Bits of bird were suspended from the wire netting. The only possible explanation was that rats had invaded from the adjoining granary and destroyed everything that moved. It took me a long time to get over this tragedy. Some particularly valuable and hard-won, home-bred birds were amongst the victims.

30
The Orchards

Although the apples in our three orchards were not a significant source of income (a few were sold one year to the greengrocer in Torrington), apple harvest time was a major event for us. All told, there were about six acres of apple trees, split between the cider orchard above Smully Ham, the orchard by the stream (with the beehive) and the orchard beside the tennis court, which was the easiest to harvest as it was on flat land and contained a wide range of different eating apple varieties. A trailer was parked under each tree in turn allowing us to reach the apples more easily. Sometimes a stepladder was set up on the trailer to give us extra height. The biggest, rosiest apples always seemed to be at the top of the tree. We had bags into which we put the apples while collecting them, then emptied them when full into cardboard boxes. Only a small proportion of the total crop was harvested, so we went for the biggest and best. No apples were collected from the cider orchard in Smully Ham because we had no way of processing them and they tasted very bitter. Collecting food for winter is a satisfying task, reminding me again of our hunter-gatherer ancestors for whom this was an essential activity for survival. It was also what a lot of animals were doing at that time of year. Squirrels, crows, magpies, coal tits and jays were all busy burying seeds, as were many different rodents.

The orchards beside the tennis court and the stream contained a wide range of apple varieties, some of them probably very old and possibly unnamed. Most of the apples we stored were Bramleys for cooking over the next six months or so. Of the eaters we stored the ones we liked best, which were the Russets (several varieties) and the Worcester Pearmains. However, in some cases there was only a single tree with its own characteristics that produced a particular taste and degree of crispiness; these we ate straight off the tree. There were 'family trees' too, where two or three different varieties had been grafted onto a single tree. We had one apple tree away from the rest in our garden, near where Lucy sat on the wall guarding the house. These apples were enormous, golden yellow and good cookers, dissolving into a delicious mush when cooked with brown sugar. We competed with each other to grow the biggest apples from this tree by putting bags around large apples to take some of the weight and prevent them from falling or breaking the twig they were attached to.

The boxes of apples were taken to the granary, where there was a whole room constructed for apple storage, with broad wooden shelves and slats around the sides to prevent apples from rolling off. Most of the apples were individually wrapped in newspaper to prevent rot from spreading from one apple to the next. In the winter I enjoyed unwrapping an apple to take to school each morning. It was a bit like Christmas as you had no idea what the apple would look like until you opened it.

Bramleys are mainly useful for cooking. However, many of these apples remained on the ground in the orchards through the winter. Once frosted, they were much sweeter, and this is when we boys would go looking for them. Maybe they were not to everyone's taste, but we loved them, raw. And we were not the only ones. This was a bonanza first for wasps in the autumn and later for blackbirds and thrushes, and especially the winter visitors, the fieldfares and redwings.

We had to keep a careful eye on the apple store. Sometimes a chicken would choose to make its nest on top of the wrapped fruit, making it less than appetising. One day I went into the store (after not having visited it for a few weeks) and found everything, the shelves, window and floor absolutely covered in dead honeybees. A swarm must have found its way in there and then for some reason failed to find its way out again (although the door was, as always, open to allow plenty of ventilation). They may have come from the beehive in the orchard by the stream. This hive was active for at least ten years, indeed the whole time we lived on the farm, but none of us ever dared to harvest honey from it. I did enjoy watching the bees going in and out, from a safe distance. They were probably introduced to improve pollination of the fruit trees.

The apple trees were also useful to us for a very different reason. Many of the trees were old and had got so big that their branches were getting entangled with one another. This was not good for the yield of apples and therefore we occasionally cut one down. I found this a bit sad. It was rather like an old cow that had spent the last ten years loyally producing calves and hundreds of gallons of milk but eventually had to be put down. This was usually because we could no longer get it in calf, or simply because it could no longer give a good milk yield. In the case of the cows, they would be turned into beef. With the trees it was rather similar, they were turned into firewood.

Few people owned chainsaws in those days, we certainly didn't. The trees had to be cut into logs using a frame saw and an axe. This was hard work, and Dad paid us boys a small amount of money for doing it. The cutting of the trees and the burning of the logs released a wonderful smell that filled the living room. We didn't waste anything. Even the fine twigs that were covered in green, yellow and silvery lichen were cut into usable lengths and, once dried, were great for getting a fire started. One year a big old and decaying tree was used for a Guy Fawkes Night bonfire. Some old and wormy timbers were pulled out of the rickety shanty town of outbuildings and used as dry wood to get the fire going, then the apple branches, including the main trunk, put on top. The fire was tremendous. We all bought fireworks in advance to add to the fun. However, the fire was the centrepiece, like a huge firework, sending upside-down showers of sparks into the night sky. Mum had prepared in advance, so we had toffee apples (made with our own apples of course), pops (see below) and potatoes that were baked in the glowing ashes. Totally magical. The smell of the bonfire, the fireworks and the food were intoxicating. Maybe this was a fitting end for the old tree, which certainly went out with a bang. Our party was effectively a wake for the old tree.

Recipe for Pops
1. 1.5 oz. butter
2. 3 rounded tablespoons dark brown sugar
3. 1.5 tablespoons of milk
4. Melt these 3 and mix over low heat
5. Separately, mix together 3 rounded tablespoons of cocoa and 3 rounded tablespoons of dried milk
6. Stir into melted mix above. Roll into small balls
7. Optional: add chopped nuts and sultanas plus few drops of vanilla essence
8. Harden in fridge
9. Delicious

31

Wild Cattle

There was an alternative way to buy in replacement cows that avoided some of the pitfalls of buying cows at cattle markets, from dealers or from farm sales. There were some specialised farmers who bought in calves and reared them right through to the down-calving heifer stage. Dad tried this source of new cows once, but only once. He visited such a farm where they offered freshly calved Friesians heifers, and he put in an order for six. The heifers he was shown were in good condition and were clearly calm animals that looked ideal.

The great day dawned, and the heifers arrived. There was pandemonium from the start. Clearly these animals had never been handled before, nor had they ever been tied up in a cowshed. They charged around in a totally demented fashion, butting our other cows and refusing to stay in a stall long enough to put a chain around their necks. They reacted to any touch by human hand as if they were being branded, quivering with nerves. We got a chain on one heifer that tried so desperately to get free that she basically did a summersault, twisting the chain around her neck like a tourniquet. Her breathing turned into strangled grunts as she lay on her back, kicking out with all four legs and making it impossible to approach her. Dad had to go and fetch a spanner to free the chain from the wall of the stall while constantly ducking to avoid flailing hooves. This was a long, long way from life as a surveyor in London.

Eventually the heifers were all chained up, but any attempt to get between one of them and the cow sharing the same stall was met by wild kicks. Dad must have been well and truly battered. The next task was to try to milk these bucking broncos. First, they were given some cattle cake as a distraction. Next, we tied a rope tightly around their withers to reduce the force of the kicking. It didn't do much good. Even when we managed to get the clusters on the teats, they were kicked off almost immediately. Not much milk was obtained.

After a couple of days of hopeless struggle and many more bruises, Dad rang the farmer and told him to come and take five of them away (just one out of the six was docile enough to handle). After some wrangling the farmer agreed to take back all six. Later we learnt that the heifers he had sold to us lived in a separate herd from the one Dad was shown and had not been handled in any meaningful way. I don't think that the books recommending a flying herd management system fully appreciated the range of problems associated with buying in replacements to the herd. At least with cattle in markets, or farm sales, you can handle the animals before making bids for them, avoiding ones that were effectively wild animals. I have a great affinity for wildlife but not for Friesians gone feral.

32

Grammar School

The last school that I attended, Bideford Grammar School, turned out to be the best. Changing schools is always rather traumatic, and I had been through this six times. Although teased, as expected, I was never bullied at the Grammar School, perhaps because I was a farm boy and consequently fairly strong. The school had a long history, going back to the 17th century, and consequently they were proud of their record as a place of learning. They were particularly keen to teach us boys to a standard that would get some of us into university.

I soon learnt that the headmaster, Mr Stephenson (better known by his nickname Drog), was the only master who caned pupils, but not often and only for severely bad behaviour. The quality of the teaching was variable, but probably in those days there was little in the way of teacher training. For example, the Chemistry master had no intention of helping me overcome the fact that none of my previous schools had done much science. Thus, he simply gave me 0/10 for my homework, putting a red line through everything I had written over several weeks, forcing me to copy the work of other students. The History teacher's policy was simply to dictate, word for word, his material (including a lot of dates), which we had to copy down and learn. There was no opportunity to ask questions or have anything explained. On the other hand, the Maths teacher, who was considered overkeen, got some of us to build a calculating machine out of wires and light bulbs, which was fun. The French teacher appeared to be in a constant state of nervous tension and was consequently teased by the kids. People threw things at him when his back was turned (conkers were a favourite). I was partly very sorry for him (he had no idea of how to keep a class under control) but also partly amused, I am sorry to say. The Art, English,

Geography and Biology teachers were actually very good, and I enjoyed their classes.

I had a constant war with the Games master. I had very unpleasant memories of Games at Belmont (which was sadistic) and no intention of participating in this subject again. After all, I got plenty of exercise on the farm, why would I need more? On my first day he asked me, in front of all the other pupils, what my favourite position was in football. My answer was none because I didn't do Games thanks to my asthma. I didn't know what asthma was then, but a couple of the other boys had successfully named this dreaded affliction before me so I thought I would give it a go. This barefaced lie worked through most of my time at the school. I did concede that my condition allowed me to play cricket and tennis, which perhaps softened the blow for him. When I reached the lower sixth form, I used another tactic. Instead of going out for games with the rest of the boys, I simply stayed in the sixth form common room doing my homework. One day the Games master came in and said how delighted he was to see me again and how was I getting on? Then it slowly dawned on him that I hadn't left the school at all but had simply kept out of sight. He was furious and said he would ring my doctor and find out for himself whether I was fit to play football. This was an empty threat. Possibly he did ring my doctor but was told that they couldn't discuss my health due to patient confidentiality. For whatever reason he gave up and never came looking for me again.

Biology was without doubt my favourite subject. We learnt a bit about inheritance, which explained how, for example, colour in cattle, budgies and Guinea pigs was in part affected by dominant and recessive genes. We looked at chloroplasts under the microscope and did heart and lung dissections of rats and frogs. I was a confirmed scientist. However, in the lead-up to O-Levels, at one stage we had to choose between different academic streams, loosely defined as sciences, languages and technical. My lack of scientific background meant that I had to do languages. I was hopeless at French but rather better at Latin (perhaps being familiar with Latin names for species helped). I was able to do General Science to O-Level and later progressed to Biology as a separate subject for A-Level, along with Geography and English. These subjects suited me perfectly at the time.

The general running of the school was orderly and predictable. Most subjects were interesting, with the possible exception (to me) of Chemistry and History. Then out of the blue we had a school riot. I don't know who organised this or why, but it was very exciting. It was at the end of term when everyone was in high spirits. We came out as usual for our mid-morning break and found ourselves being herded into the tennis courts by the older boys. The courts were surrounded by tall netting. Once we were all inside the main gate was locked and the key hidden away. We started singing, chanting and using derogatory nicknames for the masters. Masters and Prefects were lined up outside the courts calling to us to come out. At one point water from a hosepipe was squirted at us, but we could not be dislodged so easily. It started to get less fun when some of the smallest boys got frightened and tried to climb over the fence. There was a second gate into the tennis courts and the Masters looked like they were going to get in. At that point the first gate was opened, and we all burst out with some difficulty as the gate was narrow. Some of us went back to classrooms, including myself (thinking it was all over), while others marched into town, still shouting slogans. This was the bit that made everything more serious. A school riot could have been kept quiet if confined to on-site activities, but once it became public and the press had a field day then the event affected the reputation of the school. All of those who went into town were caned.

I wouldn't have missed the riot for anything. At the end of another school year, I had a rather different, but equally exciting, experience. We finished term at lunchtime on the last day, so I wandered down to the bus stop for the Bideford to Torrington run to see when the next bus would be leaving. It turned out that there wasn't one for some time. So I walked across the bridge to East-the-Water and enquired at the railway station. Again, no trains were running that afternoon. However, my enquiry was overheard by a man who was obviously, from his sooty appearance, an engine driver or fireman. He took me out onto the platform where a steam engine was quietly hissing to itself. There were no carriages or trucks, just the engine. He and his mate explained that it wasn't really allowed but, if I wasn't worried about the smuts, they would give me a lift to Torrington. I could not have been more delighted and climbed aboard. The experience was amazing. The train made quite a din, with much clanking of pistons, clatter of wheels, roaring of the fire when the fire door was opened, explosive whooshes of steam and high-pitched shrieks when the whistle was blown. Great gusts of steam enveloped us as we went along, with the countryside flashing past much faster than expected. We went through the Landcross Tunnel in a turmoil of steam, sparks and darkness, then burst out the other end into sunlight and dappled shadows. I suddenly realised that we were re-enacting the model landscape I had created. I had used a toy train that had raced around an idealised farm populated by plastic animals. It was over all too soon, and we reached Torrington station from where I walked across the common land and home.

It was a brilliant experience. Shortly after this unexpected ride, the railway line was closed to passenger trains and steam engines rapidly disappeared from railways everywhere. It was just pure luck that had given me the opportunity to have this end-of-an-era experience.

33

Butterflies, Moths and other Insects

My interest in butterflies and moths was an obsession and took up much of my spare time. I had been fascinated by these beauties since the age of about three and simply couldn't understand why my interest wasn't shared by everyone. I was in school one day when I saw a large green caterpillar snaking its way across the playground. One of the other boys simply went up to it and casually stamped on it. How could anyone do such a thing? Were they not interested in what sort of butterfly or moth it might have turned into? Why destroy such a beautiful creature for no good reason?

As a birthday present, Mum was able to get me an old museum butterfly cabinet with multiple drawers, and later I bought a second. These enabled me to build up a proper collection, with all specimens labelled by date and location. Dad had bought a small green caravan with the intention of using it for visitors (we had no spare bedrooms in the house). However, after a couple of years of it standing empty, I asked if I could have it as a laboratory. He agreed. I was totally delighted. I built into it a work surface (a converted door) on which I could lay out my microscope, setting boards, identification guides, bottle of ethyl acetate, jars containing caterpillars and other livestock, and safely keep equipment such as my moth lamp, butterfly nets and much more. It had no electricity but did have gas lamps run on propane. It was perfect for my needs and left more space in my bedroom for things like bird nests and skulls, plus cages with live birds and chipmunks.

I soon identified all of the butterflies on our farm and surrounding land (such as the Reservoir). Occasionally I would find something new further afield, like the holly blues seen on my primary school cycling trip and also on the farm of a school friend, John Duncan, in Langtree. An exceptionally exciting event was the discovery of dark green fritillaries at Braunton Burrows, near Saunton, one of the coastal places we liked to visit. These are large and beautiful fritillaries, though fast flying, and it took me several visits to collect some. I normally collected no more than four or five specimens of each species unless they were variable in colour or pattern in which case a few more might be needed. Fifty years on I still have those butterflies in those cabinets.

By contrast, moth species are highly diverse, and almost every time I set up my ultraviolet (UV) lamp, I would find something new. The closer you look at moths the more apparent it becomes that their intricate markings are exquisite and equally as beautiful as the butterflies', but less showy. Our farm, with all its diverse damp corners and patches of brambles and gorse, not to mention its straggly hedgerows, led to an equally diverse spectrum of Lepidoptera. The problem with moths (such as carpet moths, pugs and noctuids) is that they can be challenging to identify correctly. Even within a species many moths are highly variable.

I would set up the moth lamp on warm dry evenings. The UV lamp was placed in the middle of a white sheet, making it easier to spot moths as they came down near the mercury vapour bulb. I would check on the moths before going to bed, when numbers were still low, or leave it on for most of the night. By 3am there was a blizzard of insects, mostly moths but a lot of other things as well. Bats were a problem. They would zoom into the cloud of moths snatching some of the bigger insects, but I was happy for them to get their share and enjoyed their sheer speed and exuberance. Going out at that time of night was a strange but exhilarating experience in its own right, with no signs of human activity but lots of wildlife. The UV lamp was located not far from the backdoor of the house, allowing it to be powered by the mains. In the bushes between the house and farmyard there were several grasshopper warblers during the summer, creating a very strange backdrop with their weird songs. They sounded more like a sewing machine than a bird, producing a continuous buzzing noise. It was difficult to see how they managed to do this for hours on end, without an apparent pause for breath.

The biggest and most dramatic moths were the poplar, eyed and elephant hawkmoths, all of which were common, and all were staggeringly beautiful. The pink and green colours of the elephant hawkmoths seemed at variance against normal rules regarding which colours should be seen together, but they carried it off perfectly. The eggs and larvae could be found nearby on the poplar saplings planted by Dad (poplar and eyed hawkmoths) and on rosebay willowherb (elephant hawkmoths). Where possible, I preferred to rear these from eggs and larvae to learn more about their life cycles and to obtain perfect specimens for my collection.

A fourth species of hawkmoth was present on the farm, the huge privet hawkmoth, the largest moth in the UK. These never came to UV light, but one night a pair of them flew in through my bedroom window. These too are dramatically coloured. The wings are black, cream and pink, but it is the black and pink stripes on the fat, furry abdomen that appear so striking. I put these two moths in a box overnight and found to my delight that by morning they had laid eggs. These soon hatched and I gave them privet leaves from the garden. To my horror they ignored these and started to die off. I quickly looked in the moth guides in the hope that they could give me advice and discovered that they also fed on ash leaves. The healthiest looking larvae started to eat these leaves voraciously, but maybe the bad start in life weakened them because I failed to rear any privet hawkmoths right through to the adult stage. It did, however, teach me a lot about host races. The adults I caught would have fed on ash when they were larvae and were genetically adapted to only feed on that plant. I might just as easily have caught privet hawkmoths that produced larvae that were genetically adapted to feed only on privet. This split into so-called host races is believed to be an early step in the evolution of new species.

My interest in butterflies extended to tropical species, which I could buy from Worldwide Butterflies Ltd. They could be bought either as set specimens or as live pupae (which was much more fun). I was able to obtain a pupa of the giant atlas moth from Formosa, the World's largest moth (the size of a dinner plate). A few other species, including large and beautiful swallowtails, were hatched out and then, after a couple of days, liberated into the sunny Devonshire countryside. There was no danger of them becoming established as they could not survive our winter, but to see these huge Lepidoptera flying through the orchards was exhilarating. One pupa gave me quite a surprise. Instead of hatching into a butterfly, a hornet-sized wasp emerged. Clearly the chrysalis had been parasitised, and this was some unknown tropical wasp from the same country. I let it go in the end, partly because it was more than a little intimidating, buzzing loudly within the large plastic cage where I kept it in my bedroom. It was difficult to get to sleep with this metallic racket going on. This was preferable to being kept awake by rats but not by much. Doubtless it had a powerful 'sting' (a long ovipositor I later realised) and so I handled it with the greatest of caution.

Apart from using the UV lamp and sugaring branches and gate posts, I also caught a lot of species simply using a butterfly net and a torch. Many moths do not come to UV light, and so I was able to find a different cohort of species and to watch behaviour. I particularly liked the ghost moths that were only found in June/July in a damp corner of Old Clover, one of our fields adjoining the Reservoir. They are said to come to UV, but they never approached my moth lamp down by the house, implying that they simply weren't present in that area. They are a primitive species, with the hind and forewings very similar in shape and size. The males rise vertically from the grass, hover in the air for some time before coming down to earth again. It is a strange and somewhat spooky spectacle, with all these white males pogoing up and down around me in what is believed to be lekking behaviour, designed to attract females. I can believe that some credulous people might mistake these moths for fairies.

One of the primary sounds of summer is the chorus of crickets and grasshoppers. I liked to simply lie flat on the ground surrounded by their stridulations, mixed with the buzzing of bees and the whining of hoverflies. One of the biggest insects were the great green bush crickets. You had to be a little careful because if you held them in your hand they would give you a nip. I also discovered the hard way that if you confined bush crickets to a cage, they turned cannibal. There were many species of dragonflies and damselflies around the Reservoir, including the enormous golden-ringed dragonflies, rattling through the air like helicopters. Apart from Lepidoptera, the only other insects I bred were Indian stick insects. They were ridiculously easy to breed, scattering eggs around their cages every day. From the original six juveniles that I ordered from Worldwide Butterflies Ltd. there were soon thousands. In the end I got fed up with feeding this hoard and simply tipped them all into our privet hedge. I hoped they might survive for a while, because privet was their food plant, but numbers soon dropped and after a couple of weeks I could no longer find any. Probably the blue tits and wrens gorged themselves on this unexpected delight. It is reported that Indian stick insects cannot survive our winters and therefore again I was unlikely to be accused of introducing an alien species to Britain.

I was a very easy person to satisfy when it came to Christmas and birthday presents. I would simply point relatives to entomological equipment or livestock from one of the suppliers. Equally I was convinced brothers, parents and grandparents would love to receive exotic butterfly pupae that they could hatch out themselves. It took me some years to realise that their response of 'just what I wanted' was a little strained.

I had thought that I was the only member of the family with any interest in Lepidoptera, but I was wrong. On a visit to my much-loved maternal grandmother in Ruislip, in Middlesex, I discovered that she had started cultivating silkworms. I suspect she was not breeding the moths but rather buying their eggs and feeding up the larvae on mulberry leaves. When they built cocoons and pupated, she put them in boiling water to kill them. I do not know whether she managed to harvest the silk, which is tricky, but was delighted by her interest in the whole business. I suspect that the long periods she spent in India may have triggered this hobby.

34

Field Mushrooms

For the first few years that we were at Blackaton the crop of mushrooms on Hodges Down had to be seen to be believed. We all loved fried mushrooms, and when they were at their best, we were each given a plateful for breakfast – with no harmful side effects. The field looked as if it was covered in small white flying saucers or shiny pebbles from Westward Ho. They did not grow in any of the other fields in any significant numbers, which was odd. Hodges Down (next to the house) was almost certainly a very old permanent pasture and had not been ploughed in living memory. However, after this mushroom bonanza, which lasted for about three years, no mushrooms appeared, or very few. We didn't plough it and therefore there must have been a different reason for this change. There are two possibilities. Firstly, we used nitrogenous fertilizers on all our fields to increase the growth of grass, on a little but often basis. Thus, either the chemical change in the soil or competition with the lush grass, may have been responsible. Alternatively, grazing by sheep and especially horses is conducive to mushroom growth. We had neither. Perhaps this changes the upper layer of the soil, which becomes richer in humus, but why is cow dung not equally effective? If the factors behind good field mushroom growth were analysed, it might be possible to generate a high-value crop, which has the beneficial side effect of preserving ancient flower-rich meadows.

The mushrooms then were so plentiful that they could be seen from the Old Barnstaple Road. As a result, we had trouble with mushroom rustlers. These people did not ask permission to pick them, which was annoying. They came with large sacks and removed a significant proportion of the best fungi. One morning Mum could stand it no longer. She shouted at them to go away and, surprisingly, they did and never came back. But nor did the mushrooms. There were other easily identifiable fungi scattered around the farm in small numbers that we could have eaten (parasol mushrooms, shaggy ink caps, horse mushrooms, puffballs), but Mum didn't trust them and so were left in peace.

35

Livestock Markets

There was a lot more to these markets than the buying and selling of dodgy cattle. Torrington market was small compared with most but did have the advantage that I could walk down to it from the farm any time I liked. Dad took me to other bigger markets when he had something to buy or sell. The markets were information hubs where many of the farmers exchanged ideas and tittle-tattle. Who was selling the best quality livestock; who had disease running through their herds; where might you buy some good quality hay; which dealers were more honest than others; thoughts on new designs of farm machinery; advanced notice of farm sales; what treatments for mastitis worked well; which vets gave the best service for the lowest fees and where you might find the best beer and pasties, etc. And of course, who was going out with whom.

Most larger markets had huts where deals could be done. For example, feed merchants would take orders for concentrates, sugar beet pulp, straw, hay, salt licks and much more. Others sold farm essentials, such as wellies, waterproof jackets, tools, calving ropes, sheep shears, tools for applying bands to the tails and testicles of lambs or disbudding calves. Lorries could be hired for transporting purchased animals to their new owners. There was an office where you paid for animals you had bought or collected the money from sales – and reluctantly paid the market commissions.

I enjoyed most looking around the cattle pens, containing finished animals bought by butchers or for fattening further as store cattle, and the cowshed where dairy animals would be on display, all cleaned up and clipped for inspection. On one visit there were several pens of what I think were Galloways, jet-black cattle that had spent their lives up on the moors. They were long-haired animals, rather like Susie and Tina after a winter out of doors, but even shaggier. They looked very wild, and even the market men who herded the cattle round the pens treated them with caution. The worn-out ex-dairy cattle were sad to see. They had had a lifetime of behaving well but in their last few days of life this seemed inappropriate. It would have been better if they had known to 'rage, rage against the dying of the light'. You couldn't avoid feeling guilty, but what was the alternative? Preserving fields in which they could retire?

The calves were the noisiest animals in the market, except for the occasional penetrating squeals from a pig. Some may have been separated that day from their dams and let everyone know that they were not pleased. A lot of farmers, including ourselves, kept the calves away from their mothers for a couple of weeks before sending them to market to give them more condition. These calves fetched better prices and were stronger, better able to recover from the stress of going to market.

Overall, I enjoyed market day. Farming can be a lonely existence with little chance to socialise and meet old friends. Some of the farmers had clearly experienced hard lives. Some, like the Galloways, looked as though they had just come down from the moors themselves, their faces blasted by cold winter winds into wrinkles, their hands thick with the cracks and scars from pulling at barbed wire and brambles, sore from the chafing that comes from constant wetting. It was good to see them enjoying themselves on market day.

36

Terrapins and Canaries

Occasionally my deep interest in animals of all kinds got me into a little trouble. I would write to experts in a particular field with questions, assuming that they would be happy to help a fellow enthusiast. As I mentioned earlier, I had an American red-eared terrapin of a kind that could be found in any pet shop. No one knew in those days that they could grow as large as a dinner plate and predate on water bird chicks. Mine was much smaller and was happy to eat earthworms and woodlice, with the occasional piece of meat scavenged from the kitchen. However, one day, at a pet shop in Bideford, I saw that the tank containing these terrapins also contained one individual of a completely different species. I am not sure that the shop owner had even noticed. Anyway, I bought this oddity, which was dark grey with a curved, spike-like structure on the top of its shell, perhaps designed to stop it being eaten by a larger predator. Anyway, I was worried about what conditions it needed to thrive, and what I should be feeding it on. I found the contact details of a terrapin expert from my *Animals* magazine and wrote to him.

Some days later I was returning from Foxes Cross with Lucy and met Mum in the garden. She asked me whether I had been expecting a tortoise and terrapin expert who had called by while I was out. Luckily Mum found it amusing. The expert had apparently thought he was coming to see a fellow expert rather than a 14-year-old boy. He had not stayed long and had clearly been somewhat embarrassed. Worst of all he had left me no information about my strange terrapin. I can understand that he might have been a little put out. Maybe there are not many terrapin experts in the world, and he had wasted no time in coming to see me without telling me when he would turn up, or even that he would do so.

About the same time, I was breeding red-factor Harz Mountain roller canaries and had advertised some for sale in *Cage & Aviary Birds* magazine. A very self-important looking gentleman turned up in a smart suit and waistcoat. His shiny black shoes were decidedly incongruous and inappropriate in our farmyard. I kept the canaries in one of the crumbly old buildings. There was nothing wrong with that; it was the good conditions I kept the birds in that mattered, not the appearance of the building. I suspect he himself had shiny new cages and state of the art ventilation and heating equipment. He asked me the price and said that if he had known this in advance he would not have come. This annoyed me because the price was in the advert. I held my ground and told him that they were high-quality birds as he could see and hear for himself, and that I was not going to reduce the price. After much grumbling he bought a pair and left. I strongly suspect he was a big wig in the Harz Mountain Roller Canary Society (if such a thing existed), or thought he was.

For those who don't know, this breed of canary is spectacular in at least two ways. They are, like other roller canaries, renowned for their songs, which are more melodious and complex than those of most other canary breeds. They are red-factor canaries, descended from hybridisation with a red-coloured species of a South American siskin. Thus, they had bright-red plumage that was enhanced by feeding them a special food containing carotenoids. To me this made them the kings and queens of the canary world.

37

Elizabeth

Once Mum had passed her driving test, she could take me down to Torrington in the morning and fetch me in the evening. There was then a bus to take me and the other boys to and from Bideford and thence the Grammar School. The bus was shared with girls from Edgehill College and the Convent School. As my experience of girls was still almost completely non-existent, I observed these girls with some interest. There was very limited conversation between the boys and girls, the two basically kept to themselves.

I don't quite know what happened to me. I suddenly realised that one girl stood out from the rest. Elizabeth was a year or so younger than me, I think. She was slender, had blue eyes, a straight nose, pale skin and the most extraordinarily powerful smile. She was a quiet girl, perhaps with the same introvert tendencies common to many farm boys and girls, unused to too much people pressure. She lived at Glebe Farm in Little Torrington. She was the most beautiful thing I had ever seen. If a rare Camberwell beauty butterfly had been flying past, I would have ignored it if she was nearby.

If she happened to glance in my direction, briefly and completely by chance, a massive wave of adrenalin would explode inside my head. I couldn't speak, couldn't think straight, couldn't move, it was totally paralysing. Nothing like this had happened to me before. I had entered a world that I didn't know existed and had no idea what to do about it. I considered it highly unlikely that she had any similar thoughts about me. That made it extremely difficult. I was attracted to her like a powerful magnet, but clearly it was something I should fight against, but that too seemed impossible.

A problem that arose quite frequently happened in the evenings. Both she and I were picked up by our respective mothers from Torrington town square. Sometimes both mothers were waiting when the bus arrived back at Torrington, or just one of them. Neither of these scenarios caused a problem. But occasionally both were late. I would be in a state of panic. How close to her should I wait? The best thing seemed to be to keep as far away as possible. I knew that if she spoke to me, I would go red in the face and be unable to speak. That was to be avoided then, at all costs. I tried standing at the other end of the town square, but then Mum found it difficult to find me. If it all got too much, and I was getting weak at the knees, I would sometime walk out of the square altogether, down one of the side streets. No strategy seemed to work. The one thing I was not going to do was walk past her. But if I never did so, how might we ever communicate? If there was the smallest chance that she felt something for me, surely, I should take the risk? I even had a plan. I would write 'I love you' on a piece of paper and push it into her hand as I went past. It was a good plan, but I never dared to do it. What if she just dropped it? What if she showed it to her mother? Would I be in trouble? What if she showed it to her friends the next day on the bus?

I did do one rather brave thing. I was sitting next to a friend from school, Barry. In front of us, on the next seat, sat Elizabeth and another student. Elizabeth had her feet back under the seat. I found that I could reach her feet with one of mine. Very gradually I started to gently rub my foot against hers. It was leather against leather, but she could not have failed to feel it. She did not move away, which was good, but did not reciprocate by rubbing my foot with hers. Perhaps she didn't want to risk letting her fellow student see what was happening. Anyway, I took it as major progress. Possibly.

I just had to move things along somehow. At weekends I started going up to Little Torrington, a four- or five-mile walk each way. I took Lucy with me for moral support. People will often go up to a beautiful golden retriever and start talking about the dog with the owner, as I had found on several occasions. I didn't call at their farmhouse, that would have been too terrifying. But I did walk past it a couple of times, hoping that she would notice. Perhaps she would smile or wave if she saw me. Maybe she wasn't even at home on a lot of occasions. I repeated this tactic for many weeks without any result.

Then, one day, it happened. Just as I was passing her front door she came out. She saw me and went back into the house immediately and closed the door. No greeting of any kind. This was a disaster. I pitched into gloomy thoughts for many days afterwards. She had actively avoided me. Should I give up? Maybe she just didn't want to greet me if her parents were around? How ever I looked at it, I was pretty sure this was a setback.

The next two weeks I avoided Little Torrington. I did visit Great Torrington, and while I was ambling round, Elizabeth and her mother drove past in their green delivery car, probably taking milk to shops or directly to customers. As they drove past, I turned to look at them and – amazingly – saw Elizabeth turning around in the front seat to look at me too. What could this mean? She was doing so with her mother beside her, clearly not bothered that she was observed. Were they perhaps talking about me, and were they glad to see that I was not heading out towards their farm? Or maybe she just wanted to look at me? I had no way of knowing but hoped it was a good sign.

The following weekend I decided to have another try at going to their farm. On the way up there, I explored a wood I had never visited before. As I came over a rise, I surprised a small herd of deer which bounced off into the bushes showing their pale bums. This was astonishing, I didn't know that there were deer anywhere in the district. I was pretty sure we didn't have any deer on our farm or I would have seen their tracks in the mud or snow during the winter. Lucy was as surprised as I was, allowing me time to grab her before she gave chase.

Buoyed up by this encounter, I pressed on to Little Torrington. I had another plan, and it was a pretty scary one. Next to the Glebe farmhouse was a gate into a field. I decided to lean on that gate, looking out over the fields, as if I had no other motive than enjoyment of the landscape.

After only a few minutes the farmer (Elizabeth's father) came and leant on the gate, too. He said something, but I cannot remember what. I think it was "Morning". I said the same. After another five minutes he wandered off. Neither of us had said another word. So, what had gone wrong with my plan? I had simply not thought about what to say to her father if he turned up. He hadn't thought about what to say to me because he didn't know I would be there. We could have talked about farming, the deer I had seen in the woods, anything, except Elizabeth of course. He must have known why I was there, but he didn't object, which was a very good thing. Clearly, he didn't think that my pursuit of his daughter was anything to worry about. That must surely have meant that Elizabeth didn't object either but probably had no wish to talk to her parents about it (I certainly didn't wish to confide in Mum).

In the meantime, Lucy had been getting more – and tougher – walks than she had ever had before. She didn't like going through town and would go on strike, flopping down beside the road and refusing to go on. She would only catch up if I went so far ahead she could barely see me. One day I decided to come back from Little Torrington via Taddiport, going up Mill Street. This is an extremely long, steep hill, and many cars find it difficult, let alone pedestrians. Lucy decided enough was enough and totally refused to budge. She was quite a big dog, but there was only one option: I had to carry her. I was used to carrying hay bales over one shoulder, and this is what I did with Lucy. She looked a bit forlorn, and it must have been extremely uncomfortable for her, but she didn't struggle once. It nearly killed me; I would certainly never try to do it again.

Shortly after this I was back to walking through Little Torrington. One day something happened that made me rethink my strategy. There was a little boy in the road, not far from Glebe Farm. He took one look at me and Lucy, then ran into his house crying, "That strange man is back!" It sent a chill through me. I am not used to village life, and I had failed to realise that after so many visits to Little Torrington people must have been gossiping about me and wondering where I had come from and what I was doing there. I left the village hurriedly.

I had one final idea. I wrote a short note to Elizabeth, suggesting that we meet on the bridge over the River Torridge, at the bottom of the hill. I signed it with a butterfly, nothing else. I dithered outside a letterbox for at least half an hour before posting it. Almost as soon as I had done so I started to think about ways to get it out again, short of setting it on fire. This was a major crossroads, but there was no going back. I got to the bridge ridiculously early and hid in the woods nearby. If I saw Elizabeth, I would come out and talk with her. If her parents turned up instead, I would probably stay hidden. The time came and went. I tried rolling a few stones down through the woods to make my presence known. Nothing. I was just about to give up when I saw a farmer crossing the bridge. It was hard to be sure whether it was Elizabeth's Dad, but I think it was. He was wearing wellies and was marching across the bridge and up the hill towards his farm. If only I had waited in the open, on the bridge, maybe we could have spoken to each other and resolved everything, one way or the other.

And that was really the end of my pursuit of Elizabeth. I was still in love with her, and still reacted strongly to the sight of her, but I was now convinced that nothing would come of it. I thought about the phrase 'Tis better to have loved and lost than never to have loved at all' by Alfred Lord Tennyson, but was not sure whether I agreed. It was painful.

38

Siberian Chipmunks

It would probably have been better if I could have had glass panes in my bedroom door, because simply getting in and out without them escaping was far from simple. After Lucy, the two Siberian chipmunks probably gave me more pleasure than any of the other exotic animals that I kept, but they were great escape artists. I allowed them out of their cage for a few hours each day, during which time they created havoc. I didn't mind this particularly, but Mum simply refused to do any cleaning in my room. It was up to me to do it – or not do it, which was the option I preferred.

Chipmunks are exquisite little stripy squirrels, highly inquisitive and intelligent. Despite having as much food as they could possibly wish for, their instinct to store food to see them through the winter was highly developed. Thus, I would find peanuts and other food stuffed into my slippers, any old bird nests that I happen to have brought home, into any insect boxes that happened to be open and out of use, indeed anywhere that formed a dark hollow. But the place they liked best of all was the ruffles created by the tops of the curtains. If you were mad enough to draw these curtains, you would be deluged with bits of food. To make matters worse, the curtain material up there was shredded and bits of this too would come cascading down. I had very tolerant parents when it came to my animals.

If I sat quietly, without making any sudden movements, they would come and investigate my shoes and clothing, doubtless prospecting for more food storage opportunities. On more than one occasions one of them actually tried to stuff peanuts into my ears! As I had no wish for them to do this at night while I was trying to sleep, they needed to be shut up in their cage. This was a tricky business. Basically, I had to bait their cage with something particularly tasty and use a string to remotely close the cage door when they were both inside. This was not as easy as it sounds. They were terrifically active and could move at lightning speed when they wanted to. The trick was, of course, to pull the cage door clear only when both were inside, which didn't happen often.

I discovered that chipmunks, like grey squirrels, were omnivorous and willing to have a chew at almost anything. One day I left a dead zebra finch on a bookshelf (as one does), intending to study it more closely. Within a couple of hours, it had gone. Many of my other possessions (bird eggs, books, interesting bits of driftwood, skulls, pupae, etc.) received tooth marks too.

Of course, I had to ensure that no windows were left open when the chipmunks were out and about. One day I forgot, and the boldest of the pair escaped into the garden. I didn't see it for several days and feared I had lost it for good. Eventually it returned and liked to run up and down on top of one of my aviaries, probably attracted by the smell of the birdseed. I was able to recatch it using a small bird cage with food in it, again with a string to pull the door closed.

The day came when both escaped outside at the same time. I believed they would return but never saw them again. I just hope that they managed to live for a reasonable length of time in the wild before being caught by predators. Later I learnt that there are feral populations of chipmunks in many parts of Europe, including the UK, so they were without doubt capable of surviving our winters. I just also hope that this alien species does not have adverse effects upon our native fauna.

39

Rabbits and Myxomatosis

The rabbits on the farm caused serious damage around the edges of our barley crops. The barley was decimated for up to about thirty metres around each field by rabbits that spread at night out into the crop from the hedgerows and bramble patches. They were probably controlled to some extent by foxes, buzzards and the farm cats, but they bred so rapidly that this made little impact upon rabbit numbers. Lucy and I did our bit, but I doubt if we caught more than one or two a year. Lucy would find a burrow, give it a good sniffing to check whether there was a rabbit at home, then started digging. She adored what came next. She would start by enlarging the hole, digging with her powerful front paws and biting through any roots that got in the way. Gradually the hole changed from being rabbit sized to golden retriever sized. Soon only her tail was visible and even that would disappear eventually. Usually at this point the rabbit would escape through a separate exit connected to the burrow. Lucy would not notice this for a while but then give up, probably after noticing a decline in the smell of live rabbit. Occasionally she was in luck and it was a blind hole. She would pull the rabbit out and I would dispatch it. If it was large enough, I would take it home for the pot. Small rabbits Lucy gulped down within seconds.

Then, very suddenly, myxomatosis hit the farm. This is a viral disease deliberately introduced in the 1950s into France from where it spread throughout Europe. My first encounter of it was when I came across comatose rabbits with puffy eyes, barely capable of movement. Rabbit populations crashed, to the delight of farmers, although rabbits did manage to survive in small numbers. When I came across these poor creatures, all I could do was put them out of their misery. From then on we had no wish to eat any rabbit caught on the farm. The effects on wildlife that depended upon rabbits as food must have been considerable. At least the barley fields produced heavier crops for a few years.

40

Dartmoor

Our farm was located almost exactly midway between Dartmoor and Exmoor, but it was mainly to the rugged beauty of the former that we used to have day trips or go camping. Favourite destinations were High Willhays (the highest point), Lydford Gorge, Grimspound and Wistman's Wood. I particularly liked any of the hilltops with tors, the granite outcrops on the summits that had been eroded by wind and rain into sculptural forms.

Grimspound is an extraordinary place. It is a prehistoric site with a retaining wall enclosing the remains of around twenty-four ancient stone roundhouses. But it was of special interest to me because it was a good site for species of moth that can thrive in such a harsh environment. One day when we visited the place, we found numerous large day-flying moths skimming over the vegetation. Catching one, to obtain identification, was tricky in the extreme as running through waist-high heather is almost impossible. Eventually I succeeded, and to my absolute delight found that it was a male emperor moth. I had never seen this species before, but it was unmistakable. It is one of our largest moths with an intricate pattern of orange, grey, black, brown and white markings. However, even more striking are the large 'eyes', one on each wing, selected during the process of evolution to deter predators, especially birds. As it was a male, it had large, feather-like antennae that are said to be able to detect a female more than a mile away and allow the male to track her down by following the concentration gradients of her pheromones in the air. By this time, I was going off the idea of killing insects for my collection, and there was simply no way that I could destroy such a magnificent creature. Later that day, I caught a female which was even bigger and brighter coloured than the male. I released both moths back into the heather when we left.

On a subsequent visit to Grimspound I managed to find the huge caterpillar of this moth, which was in its own way as striking as the adult. It was an electric green, covered in raised cream spots from which arose viscous-looking spines. I found it feeding on the heather. Again, I let it go. We had no heather on the farm, and, like the privet hawkmoth caterpillars, there was a possibility that it would not thrive on one of the alternative foodplants it was said to consume. This was a pity because I would have loved to have kept it through the pupation stage and watched it emerge as an adult.

One year my brother Justin and I went camping on the moor near Two Bridges, near the centre of Dartmoor, beside the West Dart River. The village hosts the famous Dartmoor Prison mentioned in the Sherlock Holmes stories. We didn't see any escaped convicts, I am glad to say. We took most of the food we needed but could walk the mile or so to the village if further supplies were needed. In those days it was possible to set up a small tent anywhere you liked; no one objected.

Halfway up the slope on which we erected the tent was a leat running across the hillside. I think at one time it must have taken clean water from upstream to a reservoir or maybe a mill near the village. Not much water was running along it when we were there. It had been a hot summer and it was very shallow. We soon discovered that there were brown trout hiding beneath the vegetation that overhung the banks. All you had to do was gently slide your hand under a fish and then quickly throw it out onto the grass. Moorland trout are not very big but are delicious. We had fresh fish for breakfast almost every day.

Close to our tent was a small field with three or four horses. Now, although I am completely confident with cattle and can easily interpret their intentions, horses were another matter altogether and I didn't really trust them. One day we decided to follow a tributary river into the hills, which meant crossing the field with the horses. As soon as they saw us, they came galloping towards us. I strongly suspect that they were just being friendly but had no intention of waiting to find out. We had no time to get back to the gate and instead climbed as fast we could into a tree. The horses just skipped around below us, tossing their heads and making that lip-blowing noise that only horses can make. We were stuck in that tree for more than an hour. Luckily no one saw us.

One of the main reasons for camping at Two Bridges was to visit Wistman's Wood. This is only a mile or so up the West Dart River. I had never visited it before but had been encouraged to do so. It is a small surviving fragment of the ancient oak woodland that had once covered the moors before being cleared by Iron Age man. It was quite unlike anything I have seen before or since. The reason it has survived until now is that it is full of large granite rocks, preventing cultivation. The trees are all bent and blasted by the wind, twisted into forms that remind you of something out of *The Lord of the Rings* or the illustrations by Arthur Rackham. Even then every tree and rock were covered in moss, lichen and ferns, in places hanging down in curtains. The whole place was soggy with moisture. There were slugs everywhere, which seemed appropriate, plus lots of burying beetles, although what they may have found to bury wasn't obvious. I could have spent hours just absorbing the atmosphere in there. Apart from the occasional muffled peep from a bird, it was silent.

We camped on the moor several times that summer. Once we went to a piece of open moorland near Lydford Gorge. On the first night there was torrential rain. Little did we know it but, as a result, there was serious flooding over much of the South West of England. This didn't bother us much as we were camped on a raised piece of moorland. However, our parents were worried and drove down to find us immediately after the morning milking. I think they expected to find a collapsed and soggy tent with two shivering boys splashing about and trying to find dry land. However, they parked the car and started to climb up the hill. Soon, drifting on the breeze, they detected the unmistakable smell of frying bacon and hence knew we were okay.

Not all our camping trips on the moors went quite so well. One day, Justin decided to go on his own, with just Lucy for company.

He made camp in a new area that we hadn't previously explored. By nightfall he had the tent set up and went to sleep snuggled up in his sleeping bag. Then, at about 11pm, he was woken by shouts and hoots from what was clearly a drunken man. The next thing he knew a knife came slicing through the tent wall. The man proceeded to slash the tent into tatters. Justin and Lucy ran off into the dark and managed to find their way to some old farm buildings where they hid as best they could. Justin nearly strangled Lucy by gripping her muzzle tightly to stop her barking or growling, for their safety could only be ensured by being completely silent. Eventually the man's shouts died away, and Justin managed to find his way to a house. The kind people there took him in and allowed him to phone home. They also called the police.

It turned out that this man was known to the police and was in fact due to go to court on the charge of stealing antiques and other property from cottages on the moor. Justin's tent just happened to be beside a track that led up to the man's house. Why he decided to attack the tent was a mystery. I don't know whether he was given a prison sentence for his crimes, but I hope so. Justin, who was only fourteen at the time, must have had nightmares for years after such an attack. He never went camping on the moors again.

Maybe Sherlock Holmes would have been a useful companion on that night.

41
The Torridge

From our farmhouse the land sloped gently down to Torrington, about two miles away. But this is very misleading and does not describe the local topography well at all. If you go through Torrington via the town square and through the pannier market, you suddenly come out upon the top of Castle Hill. The land drops away steeply, almost like a gorge, to the river. The Torrington side of this gorge is covered with gorse, bracken, wild roses and bramble and can only be traversed by steep zig-zagging paths. The far side of the river below is completely different. It starts as flat agricultural fields, sloping down to the river and then gently curving upwards into patches of woodland. It is staggeringly beautiful. I sometimes got the feeling that the town had its back turned to this amazing panorama, but I certainly didn't. This 'gorge' was completely invisible from our farm.

A typical expedition into this Promised Land would start off with a cycle ride into town, where I left my bike in the car park at the top of Castle Hill. I could have cycled down but, of course, would then have had to push the bike all the way up again at the end of the day. I would then wind my way on foot down the twisting pathways using one of several possible routes, stopping frequently to search for insects and identify any unusual plants. I chose sunny days when the insects were most active and the water in the river was flashing and glinting spectacularly. The warm, south-facing slope frequently induced snakes and common lizards to bask, often on flat rocky outcrops but sometimes on the path itself. There were both adders in their jazzy finery and grass snakes, which were camouflaged and harder to spot. During warm weather in the summer, Castle Hill was covered with butterflies, particularly brimstones, small pearl-bordered fritillaries and marsh fritillaries.

However, the main reason for coming down all this way was the river itself. The water was reasonably pure and contained a great deal of life. I never saw a salmon, but they were there, and as a resident of Torrington, I had the right to fish for them. I had no intention of doing so but was rather proud in an illogical way that I had such an ancient right to hunt – or protect – these amazing creatures that spend most of their lives in the sea. Even so, I was after other inhabitants of the river.

If you lifted a large stone from the bed of the river, the most common fish that you disturbed were eels. I didn't have a net suitable for use in water. The only strategy I had for catching an eel was to lift the stone with my left hand and immediately grab at whatever might be in the hollow beneath with my right. I couldn't see what I was grabbing at; it was all done by feel. In this manner I would temporarily have an eel in my hand, but it didn't last long. Eels are covered in slime and ninety-nine per cent of the time they got away. For years I tried this strategy but was not too disappointed that they usually escaped; yet I really did want to try cooking and eating one. The individuals I managed to keep hold of were too small, but once – and only once – I caught one that was about 3 cm thick. I took it home and fried it: it was disgusting.

There was another animal in the river that interested me even more than the eels, the freshwater mussels. I had heard about the valuable pearls that could be found inside their shells. The mussels were very common in those days and so I was not too worried about opening a few. I found nothing, of course; if they were easy to find they would not have been valuable. I stopped opening them when I learned that they could live as long as we do, for 70+ years. The older ones were longer than my hand. You can age them by counting the ridges on their shells. I took some back to the farm and put them into one of the deeper pools in the stream where I could keep an eye on them. They lived there quite happily for years and may still be there for all I know.

The most exciting animal I saw, very briefly, was an otter. It was not exactly a mystical experience because I saw it from a window of a slow-moving bus approaching Torrington Station. Yet, it was exciting and unusual because the otters on the Torridge were still hunted by otter hounds (not banned until 1978) and therefore were very wary, normally only coming out at night. It briefly surfaced near the middle of the river, then vanished after a few seconds. I had read Henry Williamson's book about the fictional *Tarka the Otter* that was set here on the River Torridge and was delighted to fulfil a long-held desire to see one in the wild. Both eels and freshwater mussels are primary prey for otters, and the river was clearly packed with suitable food for them.

42
Lundy Island

Running a dairy farm is a seven-days-a-week job, and it was rare just to get away for the day. As a special treat, a visit to Lundy Island was organised. We were to travel on the PS *Waverley*, an ancient paddle steamer operating out of Ilfracombe. This was a major expedition and we prepared accordingly with a picnic and, in my case, essentials such as binoculars and a good supply of tubes for catching insects had to be packed. It was a beautiful summer's day; the sea was calm, and we were in a fever-pitch of excitement. Unfortunately, before we had even boarded the ship, this excitement caused me to develop a major migraine. My vision became blurred, I was numb all down one side and I was vomiting everywhere. We all went home again, having seen no more than a few herring gulls on the quay at Ilfracombe.

Fortunately, we had another go at making the trip to Lundy some months later. This time I had to try to keep my levels of excitement to a minimum, which is not as easy as it sounds. I tried to think about things like mucking out the cowshed, learning dates for History homework and losing my peahen that had died recently leaving the peacock bereft. It worked, and for whatever reason I didn't get another migraine and we made it to beautiful Lundy with no further mishaps.

It was amazing; I had my first sightings of seabird colonies during the breeding season. The cliffs were studded with razorbills, guillemots, fulmars, shags and many more species. Puffins popped out of what looked like rabbit holes, unexpectedly. Other puffins came buzzing in from over the sea and dived straight down their burrows without landing first. This was to evade the herring gulls, experts at forcing the puffins to let go of their beak-load of sand eels, intended for their chicks. Enormous great black-backed gulls patrolled the cliffs, taking every opportunity to steal eggs, chicks and even (in the case of puffins) adult birds. So much nature, red in tooth and claw, was going on.

I saw my first wild seals, probably my most exciting wildlife experience on the island. I don't know whether they were common or grey seals, but they looked huge, so probably they were greys. It is amazing how they can propel themselves through the water with apparent effortlessness. Somehow these big, fat animals, so slow and ungainly when hauled out on the rocks, can catch fast-moving fish.

Lundy is a working farm, but the aim was to keep the vegetation well grazed, to stop vigorous plants from taking over and, thus, encourage floral diversity. I came across Soay sheep, goats, ponies and black rabbits that were helping with this task. Not surprisingly I found the livestock and farming almost as interesting as the wildlife. The Soay sheep were particularly interesting. They are small, brown animals with horns and short tails. They needed to be tough to survive the gales of winter, but in early summer, when we were there, their fleeces were peeling off in tatters.

On the trip back to Ilfracombe, I stayed some time down in the engine room of the paddle steamer to see the enormous brass pistons driving the paddles. It had a very Victorian look to it, reminiscent of the Industrial Revolution and the age of steam. The power on display was tremendous, as was the noise.

Not long after we visited the island, the marine paradise of Lundy was horribly damaged by massive oil pollution. The oil tanker SS *Torrey Canyon* foundered and split open. Matters were probably made worse by bombing of the stricken vessel from the air in the hope that some of the oil at least would be vaporised or burnt. A great many seabirds were oiled beyond recovery, and sea life below the surface was badly damaged with effects that lasted for many years. Although I had the opportunity to make a return visit to the island, I could not bring myself to do so. It took decades for birdlife to start to increase again. Eventually they did recover, mainly thanks to successful efforts to eliminate rats from the island. Puffins are long-lived birds, as are many sea birds, living for decades. Birds that had lived through the period of major rat attacks on their nests were still present on the island when the rats had been eliminated, allowing them to start breeding successfully again.

43
Janet

The walk between Bideford Quay (where we arrive on the bus from Torrington in the mornings) and the Boys' Grammar School on the edge of town was made interesting by one particular and appealing attribute. It could not have been designed better. While the boys walked in one direction, many of the girls walked in the opposite direction towards their schools. This ensured that the boys and girls encountered one another twice a day, head on. Of course, most of the time they ignored each other (or pretended to), but the opportunity was there, if you were feeling brave, to exchange shy smiles with someone you liked. It was possible to take this a step further by crossing the road, if necessary, to ensure that such an encounter took place. Yet, it was not necessarily a simple matter to interpret these smiles. Maybe the other person was just being polite and acknowledging that, yes, I pass you each morning, so "Hello".

I started to notice that one very attractive girl was smiling at me more often and more openly than was usual. This went on for some weeks. It gave me a lovely warm feeling every time it happened, but I was unsure what to do next. I did discover that her name was Janet. Probably nothing would have changed if she had left it to me to make the next move.

Then one day I was waiting for the bus on the Quay in the evening when she simply came up to me and started talking. Apparently, her friends knew that she liked me and had encouraged her to follow me. I was totally flabbergasted. I had no idea what she said to me but did manage (in a cracked voice) to suggest that we meet up the following day (which was a Saturday), to which she happily agreed. It was so simple! Why had I not been able to do this myself? In a matter of a few minutes, I had a beautiful, lovely girlfriend!

When, in the future, we talked about that first day of our relationship, Janet had a different memory of events to mine. She insists that I came up to her first and not the other way around. Maybe it was a bit of each and that we both knew that that was the time and the place for it to happen so spontaneously.

Perhaps I should describe her. She had long, dark, straight hair and dark eyes, medium height and slim build. It's not easy to say why someone is particularly attractive to you, but whatever it was she had it. Those first few weeks we tried to see each other as often as possible. Mostly I had to hitch-hike from Torrington but occasionally was able to borrow my parents' car. I soon learnt that cars are wonderful for canoodling, which occupied quite a lot of our time together. She had a gentle West Country accent, which I liked, but she preferred my Home Counties accent (which I had spent years trying to eradicate). She wore Devon Violets perfume.

We spent a lot of time walking together, just talking. If we had the car we could go further afield. We went to the cinema, discos and live music events. We also spent time in her mother's beach hut, becoming more intimately familiar with each other, but Janet was so worried that her mother might come down to the hut and find us that we could only do this occasionally.

My relationship with Janet actually got me into a little trouble. I was officially told by the school that passionately snogging one's girlfriend outside the school gate was unseemly and not good for the school's reputation. We became, for a time, notorious. We almost got chucked out of a disco for very much the same reason. Girls at that time often wore sheer little dresses that were cut very short at the hem, and Janet was no exception. The problem was that when I hugged her (which I did very frequently) this pulled in the dress at the waist while at the same time pulling up the hem and exposing her knickers. I didn't realise what I was doing, and we had to be told off three times, and threatened with eviction, before I realised what was happening. All this was new to me, but exciting.

Janet and her mother lived quite close to my school, which was convenient. Her father, who had worked in a bank, had died when she was small. Possibly as a result, Janet was very close to her mother and vice versa. Her mother welcomed me into their lives without reservation, trusting me to be good to her daughter without feeling the need to say anything. This was a very pleasant surprise to me and, of course, made me want to live up to her trust. They invited me round for meals and for trips out in their Ford Anglia car. She even let me drive on a few occasions which, given that I had not long passed my test, was pretty brave. On one occasion I was invited round on a hot afternoon for a picnic in their back garden. I was a bit surprised on arrival to find Janet in a bikini. At one point I put my arm around her near-naked body while talking with her mother, who didn't seem to think anything of it. The only boundary I could not cross was Janet's bedroom. As long as we were up there talking, Janet's mother was not concerned. If everything went quiet, she would find an excuse to come upstairs to check whether we would like some more tea or cream buns.

On one memorable day Janet came to see me on the farm. I had been dreading this, afraid that Mum and Dad would not be as open and kind to her as Janet's mother was to me. I showed Janet some of my animals and then we walked across the farm, with Lucy, and up to the Reservoir. I tried to explain to Janet the importance of the Reservoir to me, my interest in farming and wildlife, and my affection for Lucy. Janet was a town girl and much of what I showed her was unfamiliar. She was quieter than usual, probably because the farm, and my feelings for it, needed some digesting. At one point she was bitten by a horsefly. To me such a bite is normal and of no consequence. But within minutes Janet's arm had swollen up to double its usual thickness and was, not surprisingly, painful.

All in all, the visit to our farm did not go so well. Janet liked Lucy and Lucy liked Janet, but as Lucy likes all women that was to be expected. Dad kept out of the way and Mum was polite. When Janet had gone, Mum said she thought Janet was too young for me. Given that I think there was only a year between us that was an odd thing to say, especially as Mum was at least ten years younger than Dad and married him when she was still a teenager. She also said something about Janet coming from a single parent family, which I did not understand at all. What relevance did that have?

One day I was asked by Janet's Mum if I could stay the night at their house and look after Janet while she herself would be going away. I was very happy to say yes. I don't know where she was going but expected that it was with her partner, a man who worked in a Bideford wine merchant's shop. That was none of my business. There was, of course, the possibility that I could actually spend a night in bed with Janet. I suspected that there might be a catch to it all. If Janet's Mum would have asked us to promise to keep to separate bedrooms, I would have obeyed (I hope), such was the trust and respect that I had in both mother and daughter.

In the end it came to nothing. Mum got extremely unhappy about the whole thing, and I had to ring and cancel everyone's plans. This was at a time when many late teenagers become obnoxious and behave badly, and I did my share of that. We argued a lot and I was not always truthful. Once I remember asking Mum if I could borrow the car to take Janet to see a high-brow film. Instead, we went to a disco. My parents threatened to throw me out on more than one occasion. I pleaded with them to at least wait until I had done my A-Levels and had the chance to go to university.

All of this influenced my relationship with Janet. She loved me and I loved her, but I did worry about how our relationship could move forward against this background. We never slept together, much to my regret. I think we would have done so if I had pushed her in that direction, or simply been more patient and prepared to wait. Why do we sometimes break things that are beautiful and simply good? I have to admit that I was worried that Janet did not take much interest in the farm, but maybe one visit was not enough to spark her curiosity. I could always buy her some insect repellent. The trusting, encouraging and liberal attitude of Janet's Mum was such a contrast to my own mother's opposition. How could I steer a course that kept everyone happy? If I went on seeing Janet, would my parents throw me out or fail to support me at university? Was my mother worried that Janet might get pregnant at a young age, as she herself did, effectively limiting my future career prospects? I don't know.

Maybe I should have fought harder against all these obstacles. However, Janet and I broke up and it wasn't pretty. There were lots of tears over the phone. Janet had no wish at all to leave me, and I don't think she understood why I was doing it. I didn't want to leave her either, but there seemed to be no other way out. We went our separate ways.

44

Exposure

Living as we did on a farm on fairly high ground, well away from any form of artificial lighting, meant that we had great views of the night sky and the magnificent Milky Way. The best place for this was the top of Old Clover, the highest point on the farm. The trick was to choose a perfectly clear night. I had by now a much-beloved pair of binoculars, and the first time I pointed these at the night sky was a complete revelation. Suddenly there were vastly more stars to be seen than I expected. A dark patch of sky with a few smudgy points of light suddenly teemed with white dots, thousands upon thousands of them. Best of all the vastness of space suddenly looked three-dimensional when viewed through the binoculars. I have no idea why they had this effect, but I found myself looking at vast distances, apparently with no end, stretching through light-years of space. I imagine that the brain creates the illusion that the fainter the star, the further away it must be, which is not necessarily true. If you looked directly at the densest parts of the Milky Way, there seemed to be almost as much starlight as there was dark space between the stars. Discovering this new unsuspected infinity of worlds was a profound revelation to me. Sometimes there were shooting stars, far more often than I expected. I usually managed to find Mars, the red planet. The brightness of the Moon, if present, obscured the stars in its vicinity, but the Moon itself was a wonder. The huge craters could be seen clearly, some of them hundreds of miles across. Like so many people before me I wondered how this enormous satellite managed to stay up there rather than crashing towards the Earth under the influence of their combined gravity. In fact, the Earth and Moon are a binary system, and I knew that the gravitational movement of the Moon was responsible for creating the tides. This in turn was critical for driving life on Earth as we know it. Without the Moon life may have evolved on Earth, but it would have been very different, and it is unlikely to have evolved into a boy gazing awestruck into the vastness of the night sky.

To me this was all part of the farm. Maybe all farms away from artificial lights were similarly exposed to such panoramas, should their inhabitants simply look up. For me it changed my perspective and helped me to get through difficult times.

In complete contrast, I enjoyed exposing myself to the elements in completely different ways. On the top of Hodges Down was a clump of sycamore trees, clinging to the edge of the quarry. One wild and windy night Justin and I decided to climb these trees in the dark while the wind blew the trunks and branches around. The wind was so strong that it banged the branches against one another, so we had to be careful. It was wild and exhilarating, with the wind howling and sighing through leaves and branches. We decided to go a little mad, jumping from swaying branch to swaying branch and singing at the top of our young voices tunes from TV advertisements (the sillier the better). Thus, we sang "McDougalls, McDougalls, McDougalls, McDougalls, bakes superlight, superlight, superlight, that's why McDougalls is super-sifted flour, that's why you and you and you all use it, McDougalls, super-sifted white" (I may not have got the words exactly right). This was followed by The Milkybar Kid and many other best-forgotten commercial ditties.

On hot summer days I would also climb up Old Clover, take off all my clothes and bathe in the sunshine. It was very unlikely that anyone would spot me doing this as there was no higher ground overlooking the field. I just liked to lie there, absorbing the sun's rays, feeling the gentle breeze across my body and watching the insects crawling around in the grass. I would let my mind wander in any direction it chose, allowing worries to dissipate and drift away.

Once I tried taking my clothes off in the Christmas Tree Patch. The idea was to try to get myself into the mind of a wild animal, or early human hunter, silently stalking through the trees. I soon gave that one up. There were far too many spiky pine needles underfoot, not to mention brambles, nettles, mosquitos and horse flies!

45

Bideford/Barnstaple Bay

There was a loud smack and a cloud of spray as the little fishing boat attempted to cross the 'bar'. This was a turbulent zone where the tidal water coming out of the estuary plus the fresh water from the Tor and Torridge Rivers meets the open ocean. The little fishing boat was see-sawing (or should I say sea-sawing) in an alarming fashion, appearing at times to be at forty-five per cent from the horizontal. Not only that, but it rolled from side to side at the same time. It was like a crazy fairground ride with nobody in control. The boat was very basic, just an open deck plus a tiny cabin, the size of an outside toilet. We were heading out to where the water was calmer, in the bay, in the direction of Lundy. In the meantime, we just had to hold on tight and try not to think about sea sickness. Mum in particular was looking very white around the gills and was clearly thinking that maybe she had made a mistake organising this trip for us.

The fish shops in Bideford, and perhaps Barnstaple too, had their own fishing boats. This meant that as long as you were aware of the tides you could predict when the boats would be coming back, loaded with the freshest fish imaginable. Mum took advantage of this when shopping in Bideford, bringing back the most sumptuous mackerel, whiting and flat fish. For taste and texture there is nothing that can beat a fresh-caught mackerel. It was this that prompted her to treat us to this fishing expedition. She also knew that I would be keen to see the array of sea creatures that the boat would haul up in its net.

The boat was a small trawler, picking up fish and other animals from the sea floor. After throwing out the nets, the boat trundled up and down in an area where they knew from experience there would be good pickings. A winch was used to pull in the bulging net and dump its contents on the deck. The first net-full contained a huge skate, a beautiful creature but one I would have preferred to see swimming free in the sea. Skate (and dogfish) eggs are those superb purse-like structures you find on beaches or attached to kelp. Then there were lots of starfish, scraped from the sea floor. Surprisingly the fishermen killed these by dashing them on the railing, then threw the bits back in the sea. I suspect they thought they were removing a species that would otherwise compete with them by eating shellfish. I was surprised by this as I thought that starfish can regenerate, even from a single leg. If so, breaking them up could even increase their numbers. There were also dogfish (a type of small shark called 'rock salmon' by fish and chip shops) and lots of flatfish of various species. The dogfish were skinned, probably to disguise the fact that they were a kind of shark. It is a pity that this type of fishing must disturb life on the seabed, but at low levels, where fish are caught for local consumption by small boats, such a method of fishing is probably sustainable.

Once the commercial fish had been packed in ice, the net was deployed again and the cycle repeated several times. Soon there were dozens of gulls, mostly lesser black-backed and herring gulls, whirling around the boat every time the net came in, swooping down onto the water to catch the bits that were thrown back. While waiting for the net to fill with more sea life, the fishermen got out some sturdy fishing rods and fitted them out with mackerel 'feathers'. These were artificial, feather-like lures that attracted both mackerel and whiting. I was allowed to help with this, but it was difficult, especially when trying to bring in several fish on the same line. They put up quite a fight. Again, the fish were all packed in ice to keep them fresh.

We spent most of the day out at sea and indeed could only return to Bideford Quay at high tide when it was starting to get dark. Bucking around in a tiny fishing boat in semi-darkness was a little scary but exciting (nobody was actually sick, although I admit to feeling a bit queasy). However, that was all forgotten when we came back up the quiet waters of the Torridge estuary as night fell, puttered past the lights of Instow and Appledore reflected from the water surface. It was magical. Eventually we pulled up against Bideford Quay under a deep turquoise sky.

Needless to say, we took back a big bagful of fresh fish to the farm. As usual the farm cats got their share, as did Tulip.

46

The Farm Sale

It had to come. Mum and Dad were arguing worse than ever. Mum was at art school when she met and then married Dad. I think she never really settled at the farm; she craved the company of artistically minded people and escape from the hard work and muck that was inextricably part of farming life. Dad's health was not good, and I think he simply couldn't cope any longer with the long hours and relentless work. Julian had gone off to university and so would I in a few months' time. I don't think either Mum or Dad wanted me to take over the farm; they certainly never spoke to me about it. Ideally, I would like to have gone to university, then come back to work on the farm when I had got my degree. In fact, I did move to a small-holding after university, but that is another story.

So, we followed a similar pattern of events to our arrival, but in reverse. A sale was organised, and farmers, often with their families, turned up, some to buy things and others for a good nosey around. Farm sales are very social events, and the tradition is to buy something as a gesture to a well-liked neighbour. This could be anything from a calf to a rusty old hammer. The lower orchard filled up with cars and lorries. I found it all intensely depressing. For years I had thought of the farm as a piece of the planet, along with all its trees, insects, birds and mammals, that was uniquely ours. It was a tribal feeling, a place to look after and defend with a responsibility to cherish it for our descendants. Suddenly it was being treated as a commodity, to be bought, sold and broken up. On a small scale it made me think about tribal people who had lived on their territories for thousands of years and were then displaced by loggers, miners and the modern world. Like me, they had names for most of the flora and fauna and counted individual trees as familiar friends.

A pen was constructed outside the cowshed and the cows were paraded, one at a time, around a ring similar to that in the markets. The cows were all cleaned up; their udders bulged with milk. I had known many of these cows for years, some indeed had been on the farm almost as long as we had, and it was sad to see them looking anxious and rather perplexed. It was especially sad when Susie-two came out, a large and mature cow now, which had had several calves of her own. I hoped she would go to a good home.

The sale then moved to the implement shed, and all of the machinery was sold. This included the old Fordson Major. Dad was delighted to sell it for the same price that he had paid for it ten years before. Then everyone moved onto Hodges Down, where all the smaller bits and pieces were divided into appropriate stacks. Amongst the buckets and shovels were the panels from my dismantled aviaries. I couldn't keep birds at university and therefore I had to sell them off in my own small-scale sale. It was the end of an era for all of us.

We packed the car and, as before, Tulip was sedated and put back into his cat basket and Lucy took over most of the back seat. There were no Guinea pigs this time, all had gone to the pet shop in Bideford. I took with me a seedling oak tree from Town Meadow, which was planted in the back garden of the house in Exeter. I wonder whether it is still there, a 50-year-old giant in a suburban garden.

Epilogue

So, was our ten years at Blackaton simply a bubble in time and space? We had entered stage left, with our family dog and cat, and left stage right, with that same dog and cat. Did we leave any lasting signs that we had been there? Has this bubble now dissipated, overwritten by new custodians of this remarkable piece of Devonshire? I hope that this book has ensured that the Blackaton Farm bubble has drifted on, mainly in the minds of those who lived through it. For me re-telling events during my formative years of 50–60 years ago has been a chance to fulfil a promise to my daughter Georgia. When she was small, I told her how we had rescued the buzzard from drowning, survived the terrible snowstorm of 1962, encountered the Gong Gong bird, and much more. These and all the other events happened, nothing has been exaggerated or fictionalised, and now she has a fuller picture of what life was like on a farm in the 60s, the good (most of it) and the difficult. In time my two granddaughters, Martha and Willow, may wish to read it too (probably on their iPhones or iPads).

It was time to move on. Mum and Dad bought a house on the outskirt of Exeter, and both went through teacher training. Dad soon gave that up and concentrated on his photography (at which he excelled) and gardening. Mum became an art teacher. Lucy was now a creaky old dog who spent most of her days dreaming about rabbits. I did a literature degree at university, followed by several years restoring an old Welsh cottage, keeping pigs, chicken and ducks, marrying Sarah and living the 'good life'. I went back to university and became a Professor of Ecology, travelling the world to help save rare reptiles and birds. I also worked on developing ecologically friendly farming systems, particularly encouraging insect predators to control crop pests. Georgia is aiming for a PhD in veterinary science. I never could get farming and wildlife out of my bones and am rarely happier than when I am visiting a site where I might see species of butterfly or bird, or even rare breeds of cattle that I had not encountered before.

I learnt many things during the 60s, but what really stands out is the need to let farms be untidy places, with patches of boggy land, thickets of gorse and brambles, thick hedges bursting with life, wildflower meadows and small patches of woodland. Such farms are rare now, as is the wildlife that used to live in these habitats. Since the 60s, the number of flowering meadows has declined by over ninety per cent. Farmland birds have declined disastrously, for example turtle doves by ninety per cent (near extinction in the UK), starlings by eighty percent, grey partridges by ninety per cent, and house sparrows and linnets by seventy per cent. This pattern is repeated for most of the other farmland birds, although a few adaptable species have increased: wood pigeons by hundred and forty, magpies by hundred and jackdaws by ninety per cent. Butterflies have followed a similar pattern, including species that were common on the farm during the 1960s, such as the marsh fritillary. Pollinators, especially bees and hoverflies, have declined and there is great worry that crops pollinated by insects may be adversely affected. Farmers have used large machinery to rip out hedgerows and drain wet areas. Fields on dairy farms are mostly large areas of uniform high-yielding rye grass, maximising forage production at the expense of biodiversity. Fortunately, there are moves to change the production-orientated farming systems that have dominated over the last few decades to systems that reward farmers for preserving biodiversity, help to retain flood waters at critical times of year or seek to minimise carbon dioxide production. We know a lot now about the value of pollinators and about the beetles, spiders and other predators that can help to control crop pests. I am optimistic that we are moving in the right direction and that children and adults may once more encounter the myriad of birds, butterflies, moths, tadpoles, orchids and snakes that were once so great a part of my life on a Devon farm many years ago.

About the Author

William. O.C. (Bill) Symondson was born in 1951 in Harewood Cottage near the River Chess in Hertfordshire. It was the archetypal 'roses over the front door' place, with half an acre of orchards. At the age of six he moved with his family to Chesham Boyes in Buckinghamshire, amongst the beech woods of the Chiltern Hills, which is where he became interested in butterflies. When he was nine the family again moved, this time to Blackaton Farm near Torrington in Devon. When the farm was sold ten years later, the author read for a BA degree in English literature at Keele University. Thereafter, and having married in the meanwhile, he and his new wife Sarah 'dropped out' and combined living on a smallholding, growing their own food along with renovating an ancient stone cottage in Sarn Faen near Llansilin in Wales. When their daughter Georgia was born, he went back to university, now in Cardiff, and spent four years studying for a PhD in Ecology. This was followed by 30 years of research studying the diets of insects, birds and reptiles, research which resulted in the publication of around 150 scientific papers. He now has two granddaughters, Martha and Willow and, since retirement, holds an Emeritus Professorship at Cardiff University.

Milton Keynes UK
Ingram Content Group UK Ltd.
UKHW040959121023
430432UK00004B/103

9 781908 241672